Scenes fro

SCENES FROM SOVIET LIFE

SOVIET LIFE THROUGH OFFICIAL LITERATURE

MARY SETON-WATSON

ARIEL BOOKS
BBC PUBLICATIONS

Acknowledgements

My thanks are due to the Great Britain–USSR Association in London for the loan of periodicals and for much advice and assistance.

The quotations in this book from Soviet works have been severely restricted to comply with the internationally accepted norms of 'fair dealing'. To my regret, it proved impossible to obtain permission from the All-Union Copyright Agency (VAAP) in Moscow to reproduce any longer extracts.

Published by BBC Publications
A division of BBC Enterprises Ltd
35 Marylebone High Street
London W1M 4AA

First published 1986

ISBN 0 563 20232 7 (hardback)
0 563 20300 5 (paperback)

Typeset by Phoenix Photosetting, Chatham
Printed and bound in Great Britain by
Cox & Wyman Ltd, Reading

Contents

For Cousin Joan
who liked the talks

Introduction

Most of the material on which this book is based is drawn from two series of radio talks, broadcast in 1981–3 under the title 'Soviet Life through Official Literature'. The picture of Russian life presented here has been built up from everyday scenes taken from Soviet fiction of the last twenty years. This source of information about Soviet citizens' attitude to life has been undeservedly ignored by Western students of the USSR. Often Soviet 'official' literature is assumed to consist of a grey mass of conformist writings, stories about heroic tractor-drivers or dam-builders or milkmaids – for which the authors receive State prizes whether anyone reads them or not. 'Unofficial' Soviet literature, on the other hand, means individuals like Pasternak or Solzhenitsyn, who are great writers by any standards – and colourful personalities into the bargain. These are the Russian writers who get translated into English and published in the West; and their natural successors are the recent émigrés such as Voinovich, Zinoviev, Aksyonov, Vladimov. Because their writings are uncensored, the émigré writers are felt to have a monopoly of the truth about their native land. Yet the literature which goes successfully through the Soviet censorship machinery and duly appears in print in Moscow is far from uninteresting. The quality of the writing in these stories is not invariably high; but the reflection of ordinary Soviet life, including its seamy side, is often surprising and very entertaining.

Most new novels appear for the first time by instalments in one of the many literary magazines which play an important role in Soviet cultural life. Their tradition goes back to the nineteenth century, when the works of Dostoyevsky, Tolstoy, Turgenev and many other now-famous writers had their first publication in the 'thick journals'. At the time of the Revolution the old journals closed down, but by the mid-1920s they began coming out again under other names. Today they number several dozens, mostly published by the various Unions of Soviet Writers on a regional, republican or All-Union basis, and their print-runs vary from a quarter of a million to three million copies monthly. The journals differ considerably as to the type of stories and articles they like to print: some – such as *Oktyabr* or *Znamya* – are very hard-line; one at least (*Nash Sovremennik*) has a strongly Russian-nationalist orientation; one (*Yunost*) caters for young people through stories with a strongly moral, conservative tone; another (*Druzhba Narodov*) prints Russian translations of novels written in other Soviet languages. All of them also publish long critical articles, attacking or praising works which have appeared in rival magazines. So it is possible for new authors to estimate where their stories are most likely to find a welcome and dispatch their manuscripts accordingly. Until an author can get something accepted for publication he cannot apply to join the Writers' Union and become a professional writer; so the editorial boards of these magazines wield very great power over their writers. They also play an important role in affecting the general climate of society, a role enhanced by the fact that the editors are the instruments of censorship. Just because censorship exists, Soviet publications serve as a barometer by which people can measure the political climate. From time to time a story is published which sharply criticises some negative aspect of Soviet life – the exploitation of women, the juvenile crime rate, corruption – and then all Russia discusses it, wondering: did the story slip through the control net, or is it the start of an official campaign or a new social trend?

The journal in which most of these 'new-trend' works of fiction appear, and the most serious of all the literary magazines, is *Novy Mir*. It has always been the most liberal of the journals, particularly during the 1950s and 1960s, when its editor was the poet Alexander Tvardovsky. He succeeded in publishing many works of high quality which were extremely critical of the regime – among them several stories by Solzhenitsyn. The detailed story of Tvardovsky's editorship has been told in an extremely interesting monograph by Dr Edith Frankel, director of Soviet studies at

Jerusalem University.[1]* On the evidence of many Russian writers who knew Tvardovsky personally and are now émigrés living in the West, Dr Frankel builds up a picture of him as a simple and upright man of peasant descent. He was particularly sympathetic to authors such as Solzhenitsyn who wrote about ordinary peasant types – it was important to Tvardovsky that the hero of *One Day in the Life of Ivan Denisovich* was a *muzhik*. Tvardovsky did his best to defend 'his' authors against disapproving higher authorities, but he was also a genuinely devoted Party member – and the conflict between these loyalties drove him to drink and ultimately destroyed him. When he finally lost the editorship of *Novy Mir* in 1970 his world fell apart and he died in the following year, of cancer and a broken heart.

After Tvardovsky's departure, *Novy Mir* went through a barren patch; but in the last few years it has again been printing a lot of stories illustrating controversial aspects of Soviet life. One of these, a novel by Alexander Kron entitled *Insomnia*,[2] appeared in 1977 and contains a character clearly modelled on Tvardovsky. Kron, who is now in his seventies, made his reputation during and immediately after the war with plays and a novel about life in the Soviet Navy. *Insomnia*, however, is set in the world of science: it centres round the Institute of Onto-Genesis where the hero, biologist Oleg Yudin, works on problems of ageing, and where various intrigues go on between the genuine scientists and the careerist administrators. The director of the Institute, like Tvardovsky, tries on the quiet to help members of his staff who get into political hot water; like him, he never speaks his mind in public; like him, he drinks heavily in the last years of his life when living under great strain. This director dies very suddenly, and some of his friends (like Tvardovsky's) are heard to wonder at the funeral – was it suicide?

Direct references to personalities well known in real life are rare in Soviet fiction, but real-life dilemmas abound. Soviet readers are not looking for escapism: they expect to find in novels not only entertainment, but advice on how to live their own lives. They want to read about characters faced with moral problems similar to their own: people who have to make choices, have to

*The notes are printed at the end of each chapter.

decide, for instance, how far they are justified in pursuing their careers at the expense of their principles. Contemporary Soviet authors usually make it quite obvious (just as Tolstoy and Dostoyevsky did in their day) which of their characters are making the right choices and which the wrong ones. Sometimes they embellish reality to give a story a moral ending and ensure that all the villains are unmasked: and the result is a duality which exactly reflects those two aspects of Soviet society most often remarked upon by all who know the USSR at first hand – namely, the sincerity of Russian friends and the hypocrisy of Soviet officialdom. Some of the scenes in modern fiction are taken straight from life without any prettifying; others clearly show life as the author's official censors would like it to be. Both the reality and the myth reveal much about the quality of life and the aims of society.

As a general rule, I have found that the most interesting scenes of everyday Soviet life usually occur in the less ambitious works of fiction, particularly those written mainly with women readers in mind. However long-winded these novels may be by Western standards, and however stereotyped the characters, it is increasingly clear that their authors are responding to readers' demands for accuracy as to background details. Moreover, the authors are more and more openly rebelling against the pressure from editors to produce hackneyed works with predictable plots and good factory-worker heroes.

One senior writer, Pyotr Proskurin, in a recent fragment of autobiography,[3] has written a contemptuously satirical skit on a typical scene from a so-called 'production novel'; it is perhaps worth quoting the passage to show that modern Soviet authors do sometimes send each other up:

> The building-site foreman Ivanychev – a very up-to-date, innovative chap, and moreover the possessor of a pair of blue eyes beaming with celestial purity (and a good family man to boot!) – points out to his boss, the ultra-conservative Pyotr Viktorovich Sidorov, that their new crane ought to be sited to the right, not to the left, of the building at present under construction. This same foreman Ivanychev represents a completely new product of the forces of social and moral evolu-

> tion. . . . Even when his wife overtakes him on life's staircase (she is made director of a big factory), he suppresses his natural feelings of male pride, and the very same night in bed he warmly congratulates her on her promotion. His wife reminds him that it's already getting late, and that tomorrow the burden of still greater responsibility towards the People will be upon their shoulders – so they can't possibly allow themselves any unnecessary activities tonight which might distract them from their duty. The best thing, she suggests, will be for them to separate now and spend the night in different rooms, resting in preparation for the new working day. And foreman Ivanychev, who fully agrees with his wife, . . . hastily kisses her on the forehead, picks up a pillow and quilt and goes off to the dining-room (at present they are still living in a two-roomed flat) . . .
>
> Such conflicts! The night–foreman Ivanychev's agonisings – all those torn-up sheets of paper (that damned crane refuses to be moved) – he's longing to go to sleep – and his wife's just been made a director . . . How unplumbable are the depths of the human soul! . . .

Proskurin's satire draws additional sting from his own position as member of the 'country school' of authors, who are striving for greater truthfulness in their writings.

In the pages which follow, the reader will encounter many likeable and unlikeable Soviet characters – but none of them anywhere near as improbable as that building-site foreman, Ivanychev. I have grouped the material so as to illustrate eight main themes; but I must emphasise that this book is not a complete survey either of recent Soviet literature or of Soviet life. The enormous number of stories and novels published every year in the USSR must defeat any one reader. I have concentrated mainly on the last fifteen years and on writers who are very little, if at all, known in the West; and I have completely ignored many very good writers (for instance, Chingiz Aitmatov, Vitali Syomin, Andrei Bitov) whose stories do not lend themselves to quotation. My main aim has been to show that a study of official literature, including the second-rate and the lesser genres, can throw new light on the psychology of Soviet people – of whom we in the West still know dangerously little.

REFERENCES

1 Edith Frankel, *Novy Mir: A Case Study in the Politics of Literature* (*Cambridge Studies in Russian Literature,* Cambridge 1982).

2 Alexander Kron, *Bessonitsa* (*Novy Mir* 1977, nos. 4–6). For other aspects of Kron's novel see pages 66–7 and 106–7.

3 Pyotr Proskurin, *Slovom ne ubii* (*Nash Sovremennik* 1982, no. 6).

1 Women in Soviet Society

Woman's lot in Soviet society is by and large not a happy one. The Revolution gave women theoretical equality with men, but in fact they carry a far heavier share of the national work burden than do men, and recent novels, newspapers and films are all increasingly reflecting Soviet women's resentment at this. The press is full of the problems of working wives: the hours that have to be spent queueing for food, the unwillingness of Soviet husbands to help with domestic chores, and the fact that, because mothers have to take time off when the children are sick, they miss their chances of promotion. Fictional stories by women writers contain plenty of such complaints, and those by male authors seem to reflect an increasing sense of guilt on the part of Soviet men. At the same time the stories also reveal a state of near-panic among sociologists and their politician bosses. Faced with the fact that children mean trouble and not joy, more and more Soviet urban mothers are restricting themselves to one child, or even having no children at all, and the birthrate in European Russia is dropping as a result.

All these themes are reflected in two novellas from the same journal, *Novy Mir*, published ten years apart. The first story, written by a woman, describes a typical week in the life of a young mother-of-two, a laboratory worker in a Moscow plastics research institute. The second story, by a man, gives a none-too-sympathetic picture of a super-efficient modern Soviet woman, a mathematics teacher in a provincial school.

Natalya Baranskaya's story, *A Week like any other Week*,[1] appeared in *Novy Mir* in November 1969. The author was hardly known at that time, but her story was the talk of Moscow literary circles for many months. This was the first time the true awfulness of a Soviet working mother's life had been described in print. The story is told in the first person by Olga Voronkova, and is broken up into seven day-by-day sections. The first day begins:

> Monday. I am rushing, running up the stairs, and on the third-floor landing I run into Yakov Petrovich. He invites me into his office, and asks how my work is going. He doesn't say a word about the fact that I was late for work by fifteen minutes. Last Monday I was twelve minutes late, and he had a chat with me then too, but later on in the day: he asked me what American and English periodicals and catalogues I had been looking through. The book in which we sign on in my laboratory in the mornings was lying on his desk and he kept glancing at it, but said nothing about it.
>
> Today he reminds me that the deadline for completing the tests on the new glass plastic material is in January. I say, 'Yes, I remember . . .' His eyes meet mine and he asks: 'Won't you be late with those tests, Olga Nikolayevna?' I am silent, thrown into confusion. I could say, 'No, of course I won't' – it would be a good idea to say something like that – but I'm silent. How can I be sure I'll finish them in time?
>
> In a quiet, even voice Yakov Petrovich goes on: 'Bearing in mind your interest in your work and . . . er . . . your talent, we transferred you to a vacant place as junior scientific worker, and included you in a group working on an interesting problem. But I must tell you, we are rather worried, indeed . . . er . . . surprised, that you don't seem to be taking a sufficiently accurate, regular attitude towards your work . . .'
>
> I keep silent. I love my work. I am proud to be independent. I work very willingly. And I don't think my work is at all lacking in accuracy. But I am often late, particularly on Mondays. What can I answer? I hope this is just a ticking-off, nothing more – a ticking-off because I was late today. I mumble something about the slippery paths and the snowdrifts in our new housing district, about the bus which arrives at our stop full up, about the appalling crowds in the metro – and as I'm speaking, I remember that I've said all this to him before.
>
> 'You must try to be more organised,' Yakov Petrovich concludes. 'Forgive me for reading you a lecture, but you are still only just starting on your working career. We have a right to

hope that you will value the confidence we have shown in you as a young specialist . . .'

He pulls his lips into a kind of forced smile.

In a hoarse voice, not sounding like my own, I ask him to excuse me, I promise to be more organised, and rush out into the corridor. But at the door into the laboratory I remember I haven't done my hair, and I turn round and run back along the long narrow corridors of this old building (a former hotel) to the ladies' room. I comb my hair, putting the hairpins on the edge of the washbasin under the mirror, and I don't like my own reflection. I hate my tangled curly hair, my eyes which still look half asleep, my boyish face with the big mouth and nose . . . With a face like that, why wasn't I born a man?

So Olga starts her day's work with the worry at the back of her mind that maybe her boss – a stickler for punctuality – is thinking of replacing her in this job, which she has only held for six months. On her desk she finds a questionnaire addressed to her; her six women colleagues all have one too. Questions like: the size of your family, your living accommodation, how you spend your leisure time. Olga has a husband, two small children, no elderly relatives living with them (unfortunately), a separate three-roomed flat, area thirty-four square metres. She reflects:

They really want to know everything about me, what I do every hour of the day. How many hours per week do I spend in domestic chores, playing with the children, cultural leisure – they list the different forms of this: radio and television programmes, cinema, theatre etc., reading, sport, tourism . . . Well, I personally go in for sport – running. I'm always running hither and thither, with a shopping bag in each hand; upstairs, downstairs, from the trolleybus to the bus to the metro to the office. We have no shops at home, we've been living in that flat over a year but the shops aren't finished yet.

But here comes the next question, and I don't feel like being funny any more. 'Number of working days off because of your own or children's sickness in the past year.' That hits where it hurts! – takes me back to this morning's conversation with the boss. Of course the bosses know I have two children. But how many days I sit at home because of them, no one has counted up. If they learn the true figure, they'll be horrified – so shall I be, I haven't counted it up myself, but I know it's a lot of days. Let's see: it's December now, and in October they both had flu – first Gulka started, then Kotka went sick, for two weeks I think it was. In November they caught cold – the aftermath of the flu, brought on again by the bad weather – and that was another eight days. In September there was chicken-pox – Kotka brought that home, and with the quarantine that came to nearly three weeks. Further back than that I can't remember. It's always the same – one of them's quite well again while the other's still really sick.

So what can they still get, I think to myself, afraid for the children and for my work. There's measles, mumps, German measles . . . and there's always flu and colds. They can catch cold from a cap not tied on properly, from crying when they're out for a walk, from wet pants, from a cold floor, from draughts. The doctors write 'acute inflammation of the lungs' on the certificate – they're always in a hurry, and so am I. We take them back to the crèche while they're still coughing, and their noses go on running till the summer.

Who sent this questionnaire out, and what does it mean, Olga wonders with trepidation. She consults with two women colleagues – 'blonde Lucia' and 'dark Lucia'. Oh, it's all the fashion now, sending out questionnaires, says 'dark Lucia' – and of course they want to find the answer to an important question: why don't women want to have children? Why is the population not increasing? Every couple ought to have at least two or even three children, according to the demographers. Olga's all right, she's 'fulfilled her norm' with a son and a daughter, but the two Lucias have only one child each. 'Blonde Lucia' is an unmarried mother, so no one is going to pressurise her to have more children; but 'dark Lucia' is extremely worried about this questionnaire. She has one child, looked after by a nanny, and her well-paid scientist husband wants her to give up work and have another – which will mean goodbye to her doctoral thesis. Remembering that 'blonde Lucia' has her mother living with her to look after her child, 'dark Lucia' suggests a joking solution to her problem:

'Listen, girls – why don't we arrange a triple swop? Lucia takes my flat, I move to Olga's flat, Olga moves to Lucia's. No, wait a minute, that's not right: better if Olga moves to my flat, I move to Lucia's, Lucia moves to Olga's place. Then we all get what we need.'

'You mean you want to swop your three-roomed apartment for my one room in a communal flat?' asks 'blonde Lucia', laughing.

'No, I don't want to swop at all, but – needs must! I'll lose out on space and comfort – do you have a bathroom? – but I'll gain something much more important. And you won't lose out, blondie – Olga's Dima is a great chap. My Suren will be happy – Olga's younger and fatter than me. As for me, I need a granny – oh, how I need one! So come on, girls – do you agree? Will you come to the aid of this poor aspiring student?'

A senior colleague reproves the girls for chatting in working time, and they return to the laboratory. At ten to two another colleague, Shura, says she is going off for lunch, and what shopping does Olga want done? These working wives take it in turns to have a late lunch-hour, when the shops are less crowded, and go shopping for everyone. Olga orders butter, milk, sausage, and a roll to eat in the office – to make up lost time she usually works through the lunch-hour. Then there's the crowded journey home, hurrying to get back to the flat by seven before her husband and the children get in. And so Monday ends – the first day of Olga's typical week.

Tuesday. Today I get up at the normal time – by ten past six I'm ready except for doing my hair. I peel some potatoes for supper, mix the kasha, make the coffee, heat up the milk, wake Dima, and go to get the children up. They are sound asleep: I shake them and then pull the covers off. When I pick Gulka up, she fights me and starts yelling: I call Dima to help, but he is shaving. Leaving Kotya in peace, I dress Gulka. Something is hissing in the kitchen – I left the milk on the gas – I rush to turn it off, leaving Gulka sitting on the floor and yelling with renewed vigour. The noise wakes Kotya up at last. He can dress himself, but so slowly that I can't wait and have to help him, doing my hair at the same time. Dima lays the breakfast, but he can't find the sausage in the refrigerator and calls me, and while I run out to find it for him, Gulka takes my comb and hides it somewhere. No time to look for it: I wash the children, and we sit down at the table. The children drink milk and eat bread, Dima eats, but I can't manage more than a cup of coffee. It's ten to seven already, Dima is still eating, and it's time to dress the children. 'Dima, where are Kotya's mittens?' 'How should I know?' says Dima, but he looks everywhere for them, and finds them in the wrong place – the bathroom, where he himself left them last night. I put on the children's felt boots, tie their caps on firmly, hurrying and shouting at them as though they're horses I'm harnessing – 'Stand still, can't you!' Dima puts their coats on. I dress myself; one boot won't go on – aha, that's where my comb got to! At last we're all outside. Last words to one another: (Dima) 'Did you lock the door?' (Me) 'Have you got any money? Don't be late fetching them tonight' – and so we part: it's five past eight, and I'm running again, to join the bus queue . . . This time I get to the Institute on time.

At work the other women lab assistants are still discussing yesterday's questionnaire. In the lunch-hour Olga finds them all arguing about whether a true Soviet woman ought to be guided by the national interest when deciding whether to have children. Point number five in the questionnaire asks: 'If you have no children, then for what reason: your medical condition? your material living conditions? your family situation? personal considerations? or other reasons? (underline as appropriate).' To Olga it seems obvious that the only possible answer to this question is to underline the words 'personal or other reasons'. One of the older women makes a speech about the colossal progress made in the USSR over the liberation of women. Then a cynical younger one pipes up; the whole problem for the demographers would be solved, she says, if women were paid a subsidy by the Soviet State for each child produced, as happens in France. Suddenly Olga is fed up with the whole subject: she is hungry, she wants her lunch, it's time someone went out to do the joint shopping, and she knows her hair needs combing again. She tries to bring the discussion to an end:

> 'Comrades! Let me speak, as a mother of several children! I do assure you that I have given birth to two children exclusively from considerations of the national interest. I challenge you all to compete with me, and hope that you will surpass me both by the quantity and quality of your production! But just for now – please, I beg you, someone give me some bread!'

Olga had hoped to make them all laugh, but she only succeeds in making the argument more vehement. In the end one of the senior women says, 'What are you all getting so excited about? After all, each of you chose for herself whether to have children or not.' Olga thinks over these words on her journey home that evening:

> Do we really have such freedom of choice? I remember how Gulka came to be born. Of course we didn't want a second child: Kotya was still quite small, not eighteen months old, when I realised I was pregnant again. I was horrified, I cried, and then I went to register my name for an abortion. But I felt differently from how I felt when carrying Kotya – much better. I told the woman next to me in the queue about this, and she said: 'It's not because it's your second child; it's because this one is a girl.' I went home and said to Dima: 'It's a girl I'm having, I don't want an abortion.' 'Why do you listen to old wives' tales?' he said, getting angry, and began to persuade me not to be silly. But I believed what the woman had said: I kept imagining a little girl, fair-haired and blue-eyed like Dima (Kotya has chestnut hair and brown eyes, like me). It got to the last possible date for having the abortion, and Dima and I discussed it again. I said: 'I can't murder my daughter just because it'll be a harder life for us if she is born' – and burst into tears. 'Don't cry, you idiot,' said Dima. 'Have the baby if you're so keen on it – but you wait and see, it'll be another boy!' He looked at me in silence, and then banged the table: 'Right then, it's decided – we're having another baby: no more tears and arguments.' He put his arms round me. 'Anyway, Olga, a second boy wouldn't be a bad thing either – it'd be company for Kotya.' But it was Gulka who was born, and she was so pretty right from the start – fair-haired, absurdly like Dima. I had to leave my job in the factory, which I

had only had six months (I had already been at home with Kotya for a year, and nearly failed to get my diploma because of him). Dima had to take a second job, teaching evening classes at the technicum. We had to count the kopecks and live on cheap fish and sausage . . . Did I choose all that? No, of course not. Am I sorry I had the second child? No, no, I don't want to talk about it even, I love them both so much . . .

So Olga thinks as she hurries home from work, clutching her shopping bags full of food. The family are already home when she gets in: hastily she boils the potatoes, fries some rissoles, heats the milk. The children fall asleep at the table, are hastily bathed, and bedded by nine o'clock. Her husband sits drinking tea and reading the paper while Olga washes up, then washes some of the children's clothes and sews a button on Dima's overcoat. He performs the last chore of the day – to sweep the floor and put the rubbish out – and at eleven o'clock they fall into bed. In two minutes Olga is deep asleep, her last thought – in six hours' time that damned alarm-clock will go off again . . .

And so the week goes on. On Wednesday she has her hair cut in the lunch-hour, which means she is late back to work, and again her boss notices. On Thursday she forgets to tell Dima that it's the evening for the bi-monthly political seminar, which will make her late home. She gets back at nine to a cross husband, and children whom he has fed with the first thing he could find – bread and large quantities of red caviare, which causes one of them a tummy upset in the night. On Friday she spends her lunch-hour buying all the weekend food for the family apart from vegetables – getting them is her husband's Sunday chore. But on her journey home, in the struggle to get into the crowded bus, she falls and cuts her knee, breaking several eggs and squashing a carton of milk in her shopping bags.

Still, now she has two whole days at home.

On Saturday we sleep in late. We adults would sleep still longer, but the children get up soon after eight: Kotya knows how to get out of his cot and comes in to wake us, while Gulka jumps up and down in hers, asking to be released. While their father plays with them, I prepare a huge breakfast, after which I send them out for a walk with Dima while I get down to work. First I put some soup on, then I clean the flat, put Dima's and my washing in to soak (leaving the children's until tomorrow), make some mince for rissoles, stew some fruit, peel potatoes. At three we have lunch. Afterwards Dima reads *Doctor Dolittle* to Kotya (who already knows the book by heart) while I put Gulka down for a rest. Then I clean the stove, wash the kitchen floor, wash my hair, finish the washing that was put in to soak, do some ironing for the children, sew a hook on the belt of my dress – while Dima takes the sheets to the laundry, accompanied by Kotya with his sledge. At seven my 'menfolk' return, demanding tea, and I wake Gulka and make supper. I bath the children, and quarrel with Dima because he wants to read instead of helping me.

Sunday morning finds them squabbling again, this time over money: their 'current expenses' box has only five roubles left in it, and Dima reproaches Olga with spending too much money on food. Later in the day she remembers she still has to fill in the questionnaire, to hand in on Monday morning at work. When she and her colleagues counted up the number of days' sick leave they all took in the past year – she tells her husband – her total came to seventy-eight days: nearly a whole quarter-year's work missed. Dima makes a suggestion:

'Mightn't it be better, Olga, for you not to work? You're sitting at home nearly half the year as it is.'

'And you want to coop me up here for the whole year? How can we live on your salary, anyway?'

'If I didn't have so many of these chores' – Dima looks round the kitchen, at the iron he is about to use to press his trousers, and the rucksack he just fetched the week's vegetables home in – 'I could earn more; I could get 200 or 220 roubles a month. And if you work it out, counting all those extra non-paid days you have to take off work, you're earning sixty roubles a month. It's simply not worth it, not viable!'

'What rot – I don't agree with you! What you mean is, I ought to cope with all these boring jobs on my own, while you have all the interesting work. Not viable, indeed! A capitalist, that's what you are!'

'Certainly I'm a capitalist. It's not a matter of money only: the children would benefit too. The crèche isn't good for them: in the winter Gulka hardly ever goes out of doors and she has these endless colds.'

'Dima, you know I want things to be better for the children. But what you're suggesting means simply – extinguishing me. What about my five years of study, and the diploma I got, and my theme for a degree dissertation? You'd just be chucking all that away. And what shall I be like, if I sit at home all the time? Cross as the devil, grumbling at you all the time. But what's the good of talking about it? We couldn't live on your salary, and no one has offered you a better job yet.'

'Don't get worked up, Olga, you're probably right – let's not talk about it, I shouldn't have raised it. It's just that sometimes I dream of having some kind of reasonably organised life, one where if I didn't have to run round after the children I would be able to give more to my work. I expect it's egoism on my part – let's forget it.'

Sunday passes quietly: a family outing with the toboggan, meals, washing, ironing, reading. In the middle of the night Olga wakes for no reason: she gets up quietly, not to wake Dima, and goes to see if the children are all right. She puts their covers straight, goes back to bed – and the story ends thus:

> What is it that's worrying me? I don't know. I lie on my back with my eyes open, and listen to the silence. The central heating pipes make a sighing noise, and I can hear the wall clock ticking in our neighbours' flat above us – and our own alarm-clock down here.
>
> And so another week ends, the last but one of this year.

Natalya Baranskaya's story was an instant success when it came out in 1969 – partly because it is extremely well written, with many very moving passages, but chiefly, I feel sure, because any woman who has ever worked and run a home could identify with poor Olga, while every male reader of *Novy Mir* could sympathise with her young husband Dima. Politically speaking, this novella was regarded as comparatively harmless: of course, it does contain some unspoken protest against unfeeling bureaucracy and the general regimentation of Soviet life – but mainly it was seen as an attempt to draw public attention to working women's problems. It was certainly successful in this: the issue of *Novy Mir* for November 1969 was unobtainable within a few days of publication; and since then story after story has paid sympathetic tribute to Soviet working women.

There are, however, some signs of a male backlash. Some Soviet working wives, it seems, do organise their lives more efficiently than Baranskaya's heroine was able to do: but they are not necessarily more popular with their menfolk for doing so. Quite a few stories by male authors reveal undisguised approval of the old-fashioned wifely virtues. In 1978 a long story in *Novy Mir* gave a somewhat unsympathetic picture of a successful career woman. Called *Story without a Title, Subject or Ending,*[2] it was written in rather a ponderous, heavily sarcastic style by Vil Lipatov, the Siberian writer of prose works and plays, who died in 1979.

Lipatov's heroine is Nina Savitskaya, a successful maths teacher in her mid-thirties living in a Siberian timber-working settlement. Nina's first husband, a doctor, left her when her son was aged four, and five years later she married the handsome forty-year-old chief mechanic in the timber works, Sergei Larin. As a woman whose husband had left her Nina had been looked down on until she remarried, and as the story opens she is very satisfied with her improved social status and her new husband. She has a home-help, a nubile village girl named Veronika, who sleeps on a camp-bed in the kitchen. Veronika has taken this job in order to go to evening classes and complete her education: she looks after Nina's son and cleans the small flat, but she considers it beneath her dignity to behave like a servant and dish up the meals. So Nina serves her husband his supper herself – with mathematical precision. By using her trained brain, she works out that she can manage with two trips out to the kitchen and back, and she sets the table as she knows her husband likes it, using two forks and two knives each, and fine, gold-rimmed china plates and cups.

Living conditions for the heroine of Lipatov's story are somewhat cramped: she and Sergei have one room (part of which is partitioned off for nine-year-old Boris) plus a kitchen, in an old wooden house. The whole story is taken up with their attempts to get a new three-roomed flat (with the first fitted bath and WC in the settlement) by influencing the members of the local housing and Party committees. But while the long process of manoeuvring and intrigue goes on, Nina becomes increasingly aware that her relationship with her second husband is deteriorating. She discovers that, without telling her about it, he is having treatment for a stomach ulcer, and she feels guilty – has she been looking after him properly, as a wife should? While he is away on a business trip she goes to see some friends, a retired schoolmistress and her old mother. Why am I unhappy? she asks them. The ex-schoolmistress tells her: 'You are a victim of the universal process of feminisation of men and masculinisation of women.'

But the older woman, who has witnessed the whole process of women's emancipation since the Revolution, makes the same point in a more direct form with a strong hint that it is up to Nina to do something to stop this general trend:

> 'In married life, Ninulya, it's easy enough to turn the handle of a machine and make mince come out of it. You don't need your home-help Veronika to do that. But when it comes to letting your husband be a man, not pressurising him until you turn him into a woman – that's the difficult thing, Ninulya!'

And this old lady adds that she loves watching ice-hockey on television, but can't stand seeing the European or Brazilian players kissing one another. Nina goes home, her burden of guilt towards her husband only increased by the conversation with these friends. One of her pupils at school has called her an independent woman – 'Kipling's cat that walks by itself' – and she is afraid this is an accurate description. She feels she ought to have pulled her husband's boots off the last time he came home tired and wet; she should have served him a meal, and put on a new dress to greet him. But on that particular evening she had given four lessons in school and corrected two classes' books – so she let the home-help look after Sergei and went to bed herself. But her feeling of guilt goes on mounting up. One evening she talks to Sergei about it:

> 'It's my fault you have an ulcer, Sergei! I think you love me, but all the same, I can see that you're always in a state of tension

when I appear . . . Tell me honestly, why do you always make a joke of it, when I make the coffee for you on Saturday and Sunday mornings?'

'You should just see yourself when you serve me the coffee,' he said. 'The whole of you is crying out – look, I'm bringing your coffee myself, I'm not afraid of lowering myself, I'm actually carrying it in my own hands!'

'That's news to me,' said Nina slowly. 'I always thought my face expressed undying love while I was bringing your coffee in.'

Sergei laughs at her, and Nina rushes out of the house and goes to see a woman friend. Later that evening she is looking through a foreign fashion magazine: there is a colour photograph of two naked lovers, back view – you can't tell which is the man and which the woman, both of them have equally broad shoulders, narrow hips, long legs. Nina looks at her own face in the mirror, and she doesn't like what she sees:

> A big masculine nose; a determined chin with a small dimple; a masculine wrinkle between the eyes; a square, decisive mouth; a high forehead; and stern eyes of a masculine colour – brown.

In the end the housing committee give Nina the new three-roomed flat, not her husband: he has the reputation of being a careerist, whereas she is well thought of, both as a schoolteacher and as a member of the local soviet. In other words, the authorities are recognising that she is the head of her family. But after the committee meeting, talking to Sergei, Nina suddenly bursts into tears for the first time since the age of fifteen. As the French mascara runs down her cheeks, she protests that she doesn't want this victory for feminism, doesn't want the new flat, only wants to be an ordinary wife to her husband. She wants to wash his socks and make his meals, not have him develop an ulcer out of frustration because people consider him inferior to her. 'I want to be just a woman . . .' Nina cries. If things go on as they are, she is afraid Sergei, like the first husband, will leave her. But her problem, summarised by Lipatov at the end of the story with more than a touch of male chauvinism, is that although she can organise her life with great competence, this over-assertive lady is unable to achieve what he calls the 'simple, complete, womanly form of happiness'. So the story ends unhappily and indecisively, with Nina faced by the choice between changing her life-style in order to keep Sergei, or going on as she is at present, into a future where she will be alone with her son.

It seems that Lipatov was not alone in thinking that a woman's main role should be the old-fashioned one of making a husband happy. The weekly *Literaturnaya Gazeta* in 1979 reported on an experiment being conducted by the Lithuanian monthly magazine *Sheima* (or *Family*),[3] which had started printing marriage-partner advertisements. The advertisement which received the record number of replies ran as follows:

> I am 39, average height, good figure, blonde, pleasant appearance. I was divorced six years ago, being the innocent party. I have a good life, but I miss very much the warmth of family life. I should like to find a man on whom I could lean: I want to love and be loved. I dream of a bachelor, widower or divorcé aged 40–50. I am looking for a kind, honest, responsible, cultured man of principle, who is responsive, sympathetic, not petty, who likes cleanliness and order.

When it comes to the large category of fiction which has no pretensions to be great literature, but is written simply to entertain Soviet women readers, here the attitudes to women's role are strangely similar to those found in many English romantic novels. Life is hard for many Soviet women, and you would not expect that in the daily struggle for existence they would have much time or energy left for pursuing romance. And yet, it seems, Soviet girls do continue to dream of meeting a Mr Right, with whom they can live happily ever after in a conventional family set-up. Moreover, the stories also seem to show that many Russian men take it for granted that women ought to be hoping for this sort of life-pattern.

Both these attitudes are reflected in a story by Pavel Nilin, *Married for the First Time*,[4] which appeared in *Novy Mir* in 1978 and has since been made into a popular film. The heroine, Tonya, tells her own hard-life story. At forty she was a grandmother, but still unmarried. All her life she had dreamed of meeting a man who would provide for her, but instead she had to bring up an illegitimate daughter on her own. When the baby, Tamara, was born, Tonya was seventeen, working on a building site and living in a hostel. Tamara was a delicate child, continually ailing, so Tonya had to give up both her job and the evening classes where she was continuing her education; she took night work, scrubbing floors at railway stations or in cinemas. Turned out of the hostel because of the child, she had to live for years in rented corners of rooms. Her first boy-friend, Tamara's father, abandoned her, but later she had several other admirers, at least one of whom proposed marriage. Unfortunately Tamara had by then grown into a spoilt and possessive teenager who refused to accept a stepfather; so Tonya had to soldier on alone. All her money went on clothes and music lessons for her daughter. Eventually Tonya found a small flat for the two of them: but Tamara was far from grateful. Tonya remembers how she and Tamara used to argue, and how Tamara used to reproach her for not providing her with a legal father. Tonya was mercilessly exploited by this unnatural daughter, who was ashamed of her mother's lack of a husband. Tamara would tell her friends that her mother was a scientific worker: but in actual fact, Tonya scrubbed the floors and washed up the apparatus in an institute, and in her spare time went out cleaning in other people's flats to earn the money to buy clothes for her daughter.

Tamara wanted a musical career, but had too little talent. But with the help of an old girl-friend who had done well for herself and had influence in various quarters, Tonya got her daughter into a song-and-dance group. And a few months later Tamara married one of the group's hangers-on, a would-be producer and singer named Victor. He was soon installed in the flat, and his mother-in-law was expected to cook large meals for him and his no-good friends.

Tonya is mercilessly exploited by Tamara and Victor, who want to get her out of the flat to make more room for the two grandchildren who shortly make their appearance. Tonya starts sleeping on the floor in the laboratory where she works as cleaner. Then one day her old friend Galya looks her up. She has a good job and a husband who works for the Academy of Sciences; they have a four-roomed flat in the centre of Moscow. She drives Tonya round to the flat in her car, and on the way offers her a temporary job:

> 'How would you like to look after the place for me for a while? I'm going to Sochi on holiday with my husband. And it's impossible nowadays to find anyone to do any cleaning; everyone wants to live like a lord, no one wants to do any manual work. You *must* help me out . . .'

Tonya feels quite out of place in the big flat with its polished floors, built-in cupboards, antique furniture, and shelves full of books which Galya admits are only there for show, since no one reads them. There is also an enormous dog, the size and colour of a donkey, which Tonya would be expected to look after, and which turns out to be a heavily pregnant bitch. Tonya refuses Galya's offer, on the grounds that she wouldn't know how to cope with a dog.

Up to this point, Pavel Nilin's story is just another gloomy documentary, a portrait of a good, simple Russian woman apparently doomed to a lifetime of being trampled on by all around her in their struggle to better themselves. But now comes the romantic twist. As she goes off on holiday, Galya asks Tonya:

> 'By the way – do you want to get married? Not too late? Think about it – I can give you someone's address. He's an odd person, just like you are; but he's worth getting to know. As a matter of fact, I promised him I'd speak to you, and I described you to him. After all, we've been friends a long time, and you've got a lot of good qualities . . .'

Galya gives her a name and address on a scrap of paper, and they part. A few days later Tonya writes to this Efim Emelyanovich, a furniture restorer who has been doing some work for Galya. They correspond for a couple of weeks, and then Tonya makes the journey by suburban train to visit him on the outskirts of Moscow. Efim turns out to have a wooden leg and only one ear, and he lives in a two-roomed hovel beside a scrapheap – but with his own allotment, where he grows vegetables and keeps goats. Despite his injuries, he is a handsome elderly man who has done many different jobs in his life: as a boy he was a circus acrobat, then he had two spells in prison; he has been a sailor and later an oil worker. His ear and his leg he lost in the war, which he finished as a lieutenant. After the war he worked for an old cabinet-maker who taught him all his skills and introduced him to a circle of well-to-do Moscow scientists and theatre people. Most of them collect antique furniture, and when they acquire a damaged table or cupboard they call in Efim to patch it up – which provides a useful supplement to his war invalid's pension. His first wife died two years earlier, and their two sons were both killed in the war. Now he is determined to find a new companion with whom to enjoy the rest of his days.

Tonya feels at home with Efim at once: she too is a great optimist. When he calls to her to come and soap his back in the bath, she is delighted to find he has a motto tattooed on his chest: 'Don't wait for success to come: go out and grab it.' Within a couple of days they decide to get married. Efim has an invalid car, in which he drives Tonya into Moscow to fetch her things from her old flat. At forty-six Tonya at last has a fiancé, and she proudly shows him off to Tamara and Victor – who are so impressed that her future husband is a car-owner that they fortunately don't notice his wooden leg. The story ends:

> Very soon after that we got married, and he gave me a gold ring.
>
> 'My first wife didn't wear a ring,' he said; 'they'd gone right out of fashion in those days. But now they've come back in again, and I see a lot of people wearing them – so perhaps you'd like one . . .'
>
> 'And what about you?' I asked him.
>
> 'Oh, for me there wouldn't be much point in wearing a ring – I might lose it when I'm working. I think I'll manage without one,' he said with a smile.
>
> As for me, I was so happy that at last I had a husband, that I was a married woman. I want everyone to know about it, I thought.

That story, written by the Siberian writer and journalist Pavel Nilin (who died in 1981), puts a woman's point of view on marriage as a happy ending. A contrasting story expresses a Soviet *male* point of view – although it was actually written by a woman, the Armenian journalist and novelist Nora Adamyan. Her story is called *The Contract* and appeared in *Oktyabr* in June 1980.[5] The hero, Nikolai Samosadov, is an ordinary chap who has hoped all his life for an ordinary kind of happy married life. But he fails to find it – because of his romantic ideals about how a wife should behave.

Nikolai went away to the war from his home village near Moscow, and when he was demobbed from the army he married a local girl, Faina. He worked on the *kolkhoz*, she had a job in the railway station buffet, and for a year all went well. Then one day he came home to find Faina in bed with a young cook from the station buffet. His wife treats the incident quite lightly, but Nikolai is deeply shocked. His ideal of what married life should be like has been shaken, and he leaves home and goes to live in a hostel. He gets work as a carpenter, and later as a driver, and moves away to live in town. After a time, missing his home comforts, he moves in with a middle-aged woman, Klava, who owns her own house. But every couple of months she and some women friends spend all their money on week-long drinking binges. He leaves Klava and goes back to the unsatisfactory hostel life – until one day (by this time he is over fifty) he goes to a niece's wedding in a town not far from his native village. There he meets his former wife, Faina. She has done well for herself: she tells him she has a one-roomed flat in Moscow and a small wooden shack with an allotment on the edge of town. The Moscow flat is her official place of residence, but she has let it, she says, and lives in the country house or *dacha* so as to be close to nature and admire the beauty of her own apple-trees. (She does not mention that three days a week she goes into Moscow by train to do housework for a professor's family to get the money for improvements to the house.)

Nikolai thinks he had better remarry her, and he writes to her to say as much, ending with a doggerel verse suggesting that they grow old together. Soon a letter comes back, inviting him for the weekend and including a verse from a famous poet about memories of youth and first love. Nikolai takes a couple of days off work and catches the suburban train in the hope of reviving his youth, while meantime Faina prepares for his arrival. But she welcomes his visit not for sentimental reasons, but from purely material considerations. A great deal of work remains to be done, to weatherproof her little wooden house against the Russian winter and to dig the land around it. As she stands at her front door, surveying her property, she reflects:

> 'The apples were in flower already . . . If Nikolai could see all this through her eyes, surely he would think it a heaven on earth – the rooms inside the house all clean and shining, and nature outside in bloom – and surely then he would want to add his own labour to all this. After all, a man's arms were so much stronger than a woman's . . . Nikolai's visit was a joyful occasion for Faina, a celebration such as she'd not often enjoyed in the years since they parted. Now she was hoping that his arrival would mean a change in her way of life.'

The visit goes well, after some initial awkwardness. Nikolai puts up a big shed on the allotment, Faina cooks him large meals, and together they listen to sentimental gipsy songs on the radio. On the Sunday evening Nikolai decides it is time to get things straight between them. He is prepared to forget the past and marry her again, and he offers her his savings-book, which has 3000 roubles in it which could be put towards a second-hand car for them both. But to his surprise, Faina hands his savings-book back, saying that she needs to think the matter over further. And on Monday morning she goes off to work in Moscow, saying that she has left him a paper on the table, which he is to read while she is gone. He picks it up, expecting to find some sentimental verses, and his romantic dreams of growing old with Faina take a severe knock when he reads the following:

> Contract for a joint life together, between Faina Petrovna Matveyeva and Nikolai Ivanovich Samosadov.
> Point No. 1. All money to be kept separately, with no questions as to who has how much.
> Point No. 2. The cost of food to be shared equally. Food products to be purchased by Nikolai Ivanovich Samosadov; food to be cooked by Faina Petrovna Matveyeva.
> Point No. 3. Faina Petrovna Matveyeva to be responsible for

washing all underclothes and bed linen; Nikolai Ivanovich Samosadov to wash and iron his own shirts and trousers.
Point No. 4. All money obtained from the sale of food grown by joint labour in the greenhouses which we are planning to build, and all money obtained from renting out the extra rooms which we are going to build on to the house, is to be divided equally.
Point No. 5. This joint life together is not to be registered as an official marriage.
Point No. 6. The two partners are to behave politely to one another.

Agreed by the undersigned: F. Matveyeva.

Faina's large, careful signature is already appended to this document. She comes back from Moscow in the evening, having bought food for the evening meal and congratulating herself on her good business sense. *She* is not going to be caught like one woman she knows, who allowed a man friend to rush her off to the registry office and a year later found him divorcing her to marry a younger woman – and demanding that she give him half of all her property. Marriage contracts aren't customary here yet, Faina tells herself – but that only shows how backward we still are; in all the highly-developed countries they have them. I don't need his money, I have my own: but we can have a very good life together, because one needs a man about the house. In this mood she arrives home – to receive a shock in her turn. Nikolai has gone, leaving nothing behind him, not even a farewell note. Faina, the cool-headed business-woman, is left to enjoy the blossom on her apple-trees, the promise of next summer's fruit harvest, alone.

To judge by that story romance is not yet dead among Soviet men. But not all the heroes of recent fiction stick to their ideals as firmly as Nikolai. A much more realistic portrayal of a modern Soviet marriage is given in a first novel by a Moscow writer, Elena Katasonova. This appeared in the Leningrad literary journal *Neva* under the title *Who needs a Bluebird?*[6]. As a piece of writing the novel is not much above the level of low-grade women's-magazine stories, but it gives a detailed description of the material way of life and the mental attitudes of a small group of Soviet élite: the young diplomats who are able to live abroad and buy Western consumer goods – with a very deleterious effect on their moral characters.

Katasonova's hero, Pavel, builds a successful career entirely on material values. Brought up by an indulgent stepmother after his father is killed in the war, he grows up a spoilt weakling. He studies Indian history at the Moscow Institute of Far Eastern Studies, and in his last year there marries a girl named Tanya, older than him and with a divorce already behind her. From then on Pavel is increasingly dominated by his wife, who mocks at his better nature and teaches him to stifle his idealism. Tanya's comments on political events are all based on the question: how will this affect *me*? At first Pavel is shocked by her cynicism, but later he goes over to her way of thinking. When Stalin dies, their fellow students – both male and female – are sobbing and fainting at memorial meetings in the university. Pavel is upset too, but Tanya merely says: 'Oh well, he was great, but he couldn't live for ever. Are you going to your lecture today, or are you going to stay at home and cry on aunt Frosya's shoulder?'

Like most of his generation, who were children during the war and college students in the 1950s, Pavel has been brought up to idolise Stalin. So when in 1956 Khrushchev denounces the Stalin personality cult, Pavel and many of his fellow post-graduates are knocked sideways. Their idol is shown to have committed unbelievable crimes – and those of them who were working on doctorates on subjects directly linked with Stalin's name have hastily to change subjects. Pavel's wife, on the other hand, is not bothered by the idol's shattering: she is only concerned with the concrete consequences, some of which may affect her personally:

> 'But what's going to happen with history now?' Tanya said immediately. 'How am I to teach it in future?' [She was by this time a schoolteacher.] At this Pavel flew at her: how dare she talk like that?
>
> 'What does it matter how you're going to teach?' he cried. 'You'll think of something . . . That's not the point. The point is – we all believed in him – and you keep going on about teaching history!'
>
> 'Oh, do shut up,' said Tanya, frowning. 'I know all that, and of course it's terrible. But what's it got to do with you? What are you getting so agitated for? It's nothing to do with us. We were only children in those days, thank God.'

Pavel stared at his matter-of-fact Tanya, who had worked it out that, since she was a child at the time, she couldn't be blamed for what had happened. And there he was, choking with feelings of guilt. Of course he knew the feelings were quite illogical, but that didn't make them any easier to bear.

But they settle down again together, and as the years go by Tanya converts Pavel to her materialistic philosophy of life. He has a successful career in the Far Eastern Institute: he does a doctoral thesis, and then spends several years in India as an official interpreter. Tanya goes with him, leaving their small son behind in Moscow with his grandmother. Both Tanya and Pavel now think only of acquiring as much as possible of foreign consumer goods. After three years in Delhi without any home leave, they come back to Moscow with a Datsun sports car, a Grundig stereo system, fur coats and jewellery, and enough money saved to make the down-payment on a three-roomed flat in a cooperative housing block. Now they are really able to live in style, and Tanya holds regular evening parties which their friends refer to as their 'soirées'. Katasonova describes one such evening in considerable detail: the sitting-room with an electric-coal fire and a tropical fish-tank, the guests sitting round in soft leather armchairs from Romania, sipping whisky or gin and tonic and discussing the latest foreign novels and films. Pavel and Tanya's fourteen-year-old son would change the records on the stereo, or perhaps he would be allowed to get out his electric guitar, the envy of his schoolmates, and start improvising against a recorded orchestral backing.

But Pavel is unhappy despite his material wealth. It is 1967 by now, he is in his forties, and he feels something is missing from his life. I never found true love, he admits to himself: the Bluebird of Happiness won't be caught. Ah well, he consoles himself, lots of other families exist like us, without any real closeness. I'm simply overtired: I'll think less in future, analyse things less, just live life as it comes. But it is not to be: for at this point an old flame from his student days, Yulka, comes back into his life and they start up an affair. She is a promising journalist, with a small daughter and a civil-servant husband – whom she divorces to go and live with Pavel. With Yulka he can recapture some of his student idealism. But he can't make up his mind to leave his wife and comfortable home and settle down for good with Yulka – who doesn't care about material goods, who never talks about money, but likes sitting up all night arguing with her journalist friends about their favourite authors – Bulgakov, Bunin and Ray Bradbury. Pavel has just been promoted; he is now head of his Institute's foreign liaison department. A divorce, he knows, won't do his career any good: it might affect his postings abroad, might mean he would no longer be invited to official functions for visiting foreign delegations. It might even mean he would lose his access to one of the special closed shops in Moscow, where the commissionaire at the entrance admits only those with the proper passes, and where Pavel can buy foreign records and Paris dresses for his wife. So he keeps making excuses to postpone getting a divorce, until Yulka finally walks out on him to go on with her career in journalism alone. As the story ends, Pavel and Tanya are living abroad again, in an unnamed African country, and Pavel is more miserable than ever. He subscribes to the literary magazine Yulka works for, reads her articles regularly, and keeps remembering their times together. But she is far away, his life is miserable and boring, and he knows that things are going to go on like this for ever.

The writer of this story, Elena Katasonova, has herself worked as a journalist in India and in England, and must therefore be well aware of the temptations which beset Soviet citizens privileged to live abroad. It's unusual for a Soviet writer to let a character get away with such a deliberate choice to live for the fleshpots of this world: true, Pavel has to pay a price in the form of spiritual despair – but one wonders whether in time he might get over that and start to enjoy his Datsun sports car again . . .

Much more common, at any rate in the run-of-the-mill women's fiction, is the view that love is all and material comforts are as nothing. This is the moral of a story called *A Romantic Tale*[7] by a senior Soviet writer and editor, Valeri Povolyaev, which reads like a Victorian sentimental romance but appeared in *Yunost* in 1981. It starts at a Moscow railway station, where Colonel Igor Lyubimov, a military engineer and a confirmed bachelor aged fifty, has gone with a bouquet of flowers to meet his first love, who is arriving by the morning train from Leningrad. She is Lyuda, the belle of the philology faculty at university when they were students together more than twenty years ago. Since then she has been married and widowed twice (both husbands died of cancer) and has made a successful career writing for a Leningrad literary magazine. Now at last, aged forty-two, she accepts Igor's suit and they are married. They have a blissfully happy year together, and then she suddenly develops cancer and dies within a few months. Igor decides that he too must die – apparently because their joint life was so wonderful and so unrepeatable. His friends urge him to pull himself together, remember he is a soldier, and so on – but he quietly lies down and dies. In his last moments, he dreams that he is young again, and the young slim Lyuda is smiling and beckoning to him:

> He was quite close to her, had almost reached her, when suddenly the earth gave way beneath his feet, and the next second Lyubimov felt he was flying away into a wet, suffocating darkness. At the last moment he called out her name, and Lyuda heard and rushed towards him, caught hold of him under the arms, wouldn't allow him to float away into that darkness. He reached out and clasped her, conscious of his heart's loud, mad beating. And so he hung, frozen in a state of weightlessness, hanging over the edge of an abyss, until his heart stopped beating altogether.
>
> None of the doctors were able to determine why Igor Stepanovich Lyubimov had died, what illness had struck him down . . .
>
> And yet this illness has a very simple name, the simplest one could imagine.

REFERENCES

1 Natalya Baranskaya, *Nedelya kak nedelya* (*Novy Mir* 1969, no. 11).
2 Vil Lipatov, *Povest' bez nazvaniya, syuzheta i kontsa* (*Novy Mir* 1978, nos. 4–6).
3 *Literaturnaya Gazeta*, 9 May 1979.
4 Pavel Nilin, *Vpervye zamuzhem* (*Novy Mir* 1978, no. 1).
5 Nora Adamyan, *Dogovor* (*Oktyabr* 1980, no. 6).
6 Elena Katasonova, *Komu nuzhna sinyaya ptitsa?* (*Neva* 1980, nos. 10–11).
7 Valeri Povolyaev, *Romanticheskaya istoriya* (*Yunost* 1981, no. 3).

2 Young People versus Adults

If one studies the Soviet literary journals over the last twenty years while concentrating on the portrayal of young people in stories and novels, it soon becomes clear that the figure of the young hero has gone through a considerable process of evolution, from the ineffectual idealist of the 1960s into the much more practical figure of the 1980s who gets on with living his life without bothering his head over ultimate aims or meanings. But all these young heroes have one common characteristic: resentment at being pushed around and preached at by their parents' generation.

In the 1960s, under the strong influence of Salinger and Hemingway, a crop of morally pure but indecisive young fictional heroes appeared. While rejecting the materialist values held up to them by many of their elders, these young people yet seemed quite incapable either of carving out an orthodox life for themselves, or of taking successfully to a criminal career. In the last ten years, by contrast, story after story shows young people categorically rejecting the moral code they were taught at school, and reacting against all attempts to force them into a mould by acts of rebellion, including drunken orgies, gang warfare, mugging, bank robbery, even murder.

The social climate, both in fiction and in real life, has indeed changed greatly since, for instance, Elena Rzhevskaya's story *The Force of Gravity*[1] was published in *Novy Mir* in 1962. The hero, Lyoshka, is a seventeen-year-old idealist and individualist, searching for his place in life in a small town on the Sea of Azov. He has left school but cannot find a permanent job that satisfies him. He rejects his stepfather, a dull and respectable mechanic on whom everyone urges Lyoshka to model himself. Nor can he bring himself to join his Komsomol friends in working for the good of the State. He tells his girl-friend:

> I've just been down to the port. Some of the fellows were leaving on the boat for Kamysh-Burun – they're going off to build the Komsomol works there . . . They had a good send-off, with music and everything . . . I wouldn't have minded going too – if only so many of them weren't going. It's always the same – you think up something worth doing, and then everyone goes and does it, and then it's no good any more . . .

Lyoshka thinks it would be fun to work as deck-hand on a dredger, one of those that keep the channel free for the ships bringing iron ore to the local factory. But when he applies for the job he gets a lecture from a woman personnel manager who disapproves of his long hair and narrow trousers. He fails to get the job, and falls in with doubtful company – some lads on the fringe of the criminal world, who get him to steal scrap iron for them and, when caught, leave him to take the rap. He is given another chance by a Komsomol friend, and at the end of the story, having saved his girl-friend from the criminals' clutches, is about to take to the straight and narrow. He sits on a street bench, thinking things over:

> He could always go to the Virgin Lands, like those students yesterday – his stepfather would praise him if he did that – but he had no wish to live by *that* dreary chap's rules of life. The point was, he needed to find his own destiny in life, whether he went East or started work in a factory. What sort of human being was he? What did he want? Why had he been born? He decided to sit there till morning if necessary, and not to go anywhere until he understood things.

However much he tries to conform, Lyoshka is never going to make a successful career, and he will always be a misfit in Soviet society. The same is true of the hero of a story published in 1964, *One Day without Lies*.[2] The author, Viktoria Tokareva, was at that time still a student at the Moscow Cinema Institute. Her hero, Valya, is a secondary-school French teacher aged twenty-five, bored both with his job and with his girl-friend. But unlike Rzhevskaya's hero Lyoshka, Valya one day wakes up and resolves to make a small personal protest. This is how Tokareva's story starts:

> Last night I dreamt of a rainbow. I was standing by a lake, and the rainbow was reflected in the water, so that it was as though I was between two rainbows, one above me and the other below. I had a feeling of utter happiness, like one gets only in dreams, never in real life – in real life there is always something lacking . . . It occurred to me that recently I have been telling too many lies, both necessary and unnecessary ones, and usually about small things, which is a bad sign. It means I don't feel free, I must be afraid of someone – people always lie when they are afraid. So I put my trousers on, and decided that today I would not be afraid of anyone.

The only result of this decision is that Valya has a really terrible day. In the first place, through dreaming about that rainbow, he overslept, with the result that he is late starting out for school. Then on the trolleybus, where the fare is four kopecks, he finds in his pocket three one-kopeck pieces and one five-kopeck piece, puts the three kopecks into the fares-box and helps himself to a ticket – and gets severely ticked off by a woman inspector. At school he has a class of twelve-year-olds to whom he is meant to be teaching French strictly according to the syllabus. Instead he talks to them about linguistics:

> I got up from behind the table and started telling them about the French language in general – not about the forms of the verbs, but about what interests me: about phonetics, about why it is that a foreigner who has learnt Russian still speaks with an accent; about the art of literary translation, about how you can translate the same phrase in different ways. I read them bits from Lyubimov's translation of Rabelais. It was the first time those kids had ever heard any Rabelais, and I watched how they listened to it: some propped their chins on their fists, some leant back and looked out of the window at the sky . . . There they were sitting in front of me, thirty different individuals, and until

that moment they had all struck me as being as alike as peas in a pod . . . Then the bell went; the lesson was over, and I hadn't explained the imperfect tense in verbs of the first group. In other words, I was lagging behind the syllabus, and that meant plenty to talk about at the next teachers' council meeting . . .

The next event in Valya's day is lunch in the school canteen. He is still determined to spend the day fearlessly speaking the truth: it is his bad luck that the headmistress, Vera Petrovna, sits down at his table. When she reproaches him with having arrived late for the third time that week, he corrects her – it was actually the fourth time – and when she asks, isn't he ashamed of himself, he replies, 'No, not very.' He then admits that he never wanted to be a schoolteacher, and that his ambition is to write stories, but that so far no magazine has agreed to print them. Only the bell for the start of his next class saves him from making further revelations destructive of his image as a promising language instructor. And when after work he goes to see his girl-friend, Nina, his frankness gets him into further trouble. His true explanation of why he was late for their date is not believed; and when Nina's mother serves the supper and he is asked how he likes the soup, no one is pleased when he makes a face and says, 'It's all right, I suppose.' The story ends with Valya summing up, with characteristic dry humour, the results of his one day without lies:

> I had spent the day just as I wanted to, not being afraid of anyone, and saying exactly what I thought. It's true that everyone had looked surprised, but they had all been nice to me . . . The advantages of today were quite obvious to me. But at the same time I realised that if I were to repeat it tomorrow, the bus inspector would certainly fine me, Vera Petrovna would sack me, and Nina would turn me out of the house. So it seems that you can only speak the truth if you live by the truth.

The heroes of both those stories from the 1960s are rebels against the compulsory falsehoods of Soviet life, against the double-talk and the lip-service which has to be paid to goals in which no one any longer believes, particularly the perfect communist society of the future. Other heroes going through a phase of youthful rebellion against their elders' conservatism are to be found in the early stories by Andrei Bitov, Anatoli Kuznetsov and Vasili Aksyonov.

Aksyonov in particular, in his first stories written long before his emigration to the West, depicted restless young people who seek a better way of life and are determined not to accept their values at second-hand. In the story *Ticket to the Stars*[3] for instance (1961), Dimka, a lad of seventeen, tells his elder brother: 'I'd rather be a tramp suffering privation, than live my whole life as a boy doing only what other people want me to do.' Aksyonov's early heroes are rebels not only against the adults who want to direct their lives, but against the greyness and the narrow limitations of Soviet life in general. The hero of *Halfway to the Moon*[4] (1962) is a young truck driver, Valeri Kirpichenko, who spends eleven months of every year transporting loads of timber on the island of Sakhalin. He earns a lot of money, but lives a hard, boring life in primitive conditions, hoping one day to find something better – a higher form of life, a bit nearer to the moon. On his annual holiday, he usually flies south to the Black Sea sun and spends his earnings on drink and girls. This time, sobering up after a preliminary orgy in Krasnoyarsk, he decides to fly first to Moscow, to buy himself some clothes. But in the plane, he suddenly falls in love:

> 'May I take your coat?' asked the stewardess. Kirpichenko glanced at her and was struck dumb. She was smiling. Her smiling face and her hair were bent over him – she had dark hair, not black but dark, and doubtless soft to the touch; it was styled to look dense – like fur, like nylon, like all the wonders of the world. Her fingers touched the sheepskin of his coat, and he had never seen fingers like hers before. Girls like that only come in magazines – well, perhaps they do exist in real life as well, but there had never been such a girl before, not with a smile like that, and speaking in the voice of the first woman ever to live on this earth . . .

All he ever discovers about this stewardess is that her name is Tanya and she lives in Moscow. The plane lands, he goes to GUM and buys three suits – and then returns to the airport and spends the rest of his holiday flying to and fro between Moscow and Khabarovsk, hoping with every plane that Tanya will be among the crew. She never is. Valeri only once catches a glimpse of her, on the ground at an airport, chatting to a group of other stewardesses. But he is blissfully happy just in the knowledge that she exists: he wears his new suits one after another, reads more books and does more thinking than ever before. It is the best holiday he has had in his life. He looks out of a plane's porthole, and the moon doesn't seem at all far away: it feels as though he were halfway there . . .

In all these stories the young people may rebel against the details of their hard or boring lives, but they never criticise the system as such, and indeed one feels that after a spell of rebellion, they will probably all settle down to become middle-aged pillars of the Establishment. Perhaps the most attractive character among these young heroes is Senya Shalai, the trawler deck-hand from Georgi Vladimov's *Three Minutes' Silence*,[5] a novel of high literary quality which appeared in *Novy Mir* in 1969. This was six years before Vladimov became classified as a 'dissident' writer as a result of the publication in the West of his story about a Stalinist camp guard-dog, *Faithful Ruslan*. Vladimov is now in emigration, but in 1969 he was still writing for publication in the Soviet 'thick journals'.

Senya Shalai is a twenty-five-year-old from a village in central Russia, who signed on in the Northern fishing fleet because the pay was good, and who then got hooked on the fisherman's life. When the story starts, he has been three years on the trawlers, and although he is always talking of leaving, somehow he always signs on for one more trip after the herring. He falls in with evil company – two of the so-called 'beach boys' or layabouts, who hang about the port waiting to latch on to anyone coming off a boat and collecting several months' pay after a long trip. Senya is caught and fleeced by the 'beach boys', losing all the money he planned to spend on starting a new life ashore. On his next trip, however, he meets two young first-timers who are not in the fishing fleet for money, and who still have a romantic idea of the reality of the Soviet working man's life. Senya soon makes friends with one of these lads, Alik, a student from a fisheries research institute:

> 'You find it hard, the life on board?'
> 'Oh no – I've never felt so good. The harder the better.'

'Good for you!'

'It's true, what I'm saying. Sooner or later you have to find yourself, and my life so far has been an awful one.'

'How was it awful?'

'Not what you think – no one in my family has been in prison, and they're all alive, thank God. But everything has always been so easy: ten years going to and fro from school – two blocks away from home, there and back every day. Then along the same road to the Institute; then to another Institute. Living like that, you can choke with all the information you absorb, and you'll never see Easter Island, or the Tahitian girls dancing – except in the cinema – and you'll never sit there with a garland round your neck, made for you by the chief's daughter.'

'You know, I'll never see that either before I die.'

'No, but you'll have lived. At least one day a week is carved into your memory – because a man remembers the days when things were bad, when he was hungry, or lying in a trench, or sharing a cigarette between three of you and getting the butt-end. Living in a warm flat, with a bathroom and WC – that's fine, of course, but there's nothing worth remembering . . .'

'Will you go back to your Institute after this trip?'

'Yes, of course – where else would I go? I took some "sabbatical leave" – that's what they call it, and usually it's an excuse to do nothing. But this time I'll be able to say: I've sailed with the trawler fleet . . .'

Alik knows he has a secure research job to go back to, and is in no doubt as to what his future will be like. But what of Vladimov's hero, Senya, who has had no higher education? How does he see his future? Senya is befriended by the chief mechanic on board his trawler, who treats him like a son and whom Senya calls affectionately 'grandpa'. As he lies on his bunk during a storm, Senya builds up this picture of a future life ashore, together with 'grandpa':

> How good it would be if we could settle down somewhere together. He would complete his last voyage, and so would I, and we would take our two women and go somewhere in Russia, somewhere where there's grass and forest and a river

nearby. There's a good place like that near Oryol, just what we'd need. Then we'd build ourselves a wooden house, and I'd get my mother to join us from the town – the old girl's lived alone long enough. We could have a wonderful life, all together. There's always work to be found: if all else fails, there's the timber-floating on the Oka. But what would be really good would be if grandpa and I could run a river steamer, taking tourists up and down the river and showing them the churches and the old battlefields. Grandpa would be the captain and the mechanic, and I'd cast off and make fast and take the tickets and look after the boat in general. I'd have time to read – there's so much I've not read yet! And grandpa would be able to see my children – I'll certainly have some kids one day – and I would teach them how to understand life, they wouldn't play the fool with me . . . And why shouldn't all this happen? It's only necessary to want it enough. I've got plenty of energy: I just need to know what it is I want . . .

Senya does not get much time for such daydreaming on this trip, for everything goes wrong. The trawler, which is an old vessel on its last voyage before being scrapped, starts out with a leak which gets rapidly worse in the bad weather, and the engine is defective and only running at half-speed despite the loving care lavished upon it by the old mechanic. They are swept helplessly towards the inhospitable cliffs of the Faroe Islands. Their SOS calls are received by their Soviet base-ship, which sends two tugs to their aid, but they cannot possibly arrive in time. As the inevitable shipwreck approaches, they meet up with a Scottish trawler, the *Girl Peggy* from Aberdeen, which seems to be in a worse plight than their own, and they rescue her crew of four. But now the cliffs are looming up – they hit a rock with an impact which breaks the mast and flings Senya to his knees on the deck, where he cries out, 'If you're up there, then save us!' – and his prayer is answered. The waves carry them, not on to the rocks, but through a narrow opening into a fjord, where they are able to make the necessary repairs while the storm abates. So the story ends happily, with a banquet on board the base-ship for the rescued Scottish fishermen, and with Senya deciding to stay with the trawler fleet, although at the start of the story he had firmly decided it was time to quit this life. A large part of his motive for doing this seems to be the feeling of comradeship between sailors of all nations, which was strengthened in him by the incident of rescuing the *Girl Peggy*'s crew during the storm. He himself sums up his philosophy like this: 'If we had three minutes a day, every day, in which to be quiet, to listen, to help someone – then gradually we'd all become human beings.'

At one point during the story, when the storm is at its height and he realises that they are probably all doomed, Senya recalls his favourite episode from his years with the trawler fleet. It was perhaps the happiest incident of his life, and it concerned a baby whale. This is one of the real 'gems' of Soviet literature of the last twenty years. It is beautifully written, in everyday modern Russian; it has been polished and cut by the author – there are no superfluous passages; and it expresses one of the most attractive traits of Soviet young people – the longing to get out and do something positive to set the world to rights, and to do it together, without national divisions:

> . . . I don't know how it happened that he got into our nets: whales don't eat our herring like the sharks do. But anyway, this was quite a young one – perhaps he had lost his mother, gone mad with fright and rushed to and fro through the sea until he got himself all tangled up . . . His weight was pulling our trawler around . . . We couldn't get rid of him without cutting the nets, and this we didn't want to do – besides, the whale would have died then, he was so entangled that he couldn't swim . . . So we hauled him aboard, using all the cranes and manpower we had – tail first, and we put him across the deck, his head on one side of the boat and his tail the other. Then we disentangled him from the nets, while he lay quite still, just his tail jerking from time to time . . . Someone had the idea to pour sea-water over him so that his skin would not dry out, and one of the deck-hands was given this duty. Then the little whale quieted down, just making a gentle whistling noise. He was a beautiful colour, dark blue on top and gradually lighter down to his stomach. And the surprising thing was that, although all sea creatures are usually cold, if you touched this one, it was like stroking a horse on its muzzle, near the nostrils.

So what were we going to do with him? We had him disentangled, but how were we going to get him back into the sea? We didn't have a powerful enough crane. Meanwhile all work on board had to stop because the whole deck was occupied by the whale – we couldn't get from the bow to the stern. Some of us tried crawling over him, but he got agitated and threw them off, so we had to build a special plank walkway over him . . . Someone said: 'Let's take him back to the base-ship and hand him in instead of the herring we ought to be catching; he must weigh eight tons, and he's spoilt our plan fulfilment, so let *him* make good the shortfall.'

But meanwhile all the other fishing-boats around us had noticed that we had a whale on board, and radio signals kept coming in asking: 'Where are you taking the whale? Don't you know the international conventions, and that it's not allowed to hunt whales so young?' We'd forgotten about the conventions, since we never went after whales. But willy-nilly we had to take our whale to the base-ship; there was no way we could get rid of him without their help. And the nearer we got to the base-ship, the more foreign vessels gathered round us – Norwegians, French, English, Faroese, about eighty of them in all – everyone forgot about the herring and thought only of the whale. And the whale just lay there whistling, not knowing anything about any conventions. When we got near the base-ship, a Norwegian cruiser came out to meet us and three helicopters were hovering overhead, photographing us from the air. The cruiser sent an order: 'Put the whale back in the sea at once.' 'That's what we want to do, but we can't.' 'How did it get on board?' 'We can't understand it ourselves!'

I well remember that morning when we docked at the base-ship. It was a flat calm, the breeze hardly moving the bunting on the masts: blue sky, blue water, the sun shining like July in the Crimea. And the whole sea covered with ships of all flags, all colours, and the helicopters still overhead. They passed us a line from the base-ship, and we tied it with a reef knot round the whale's tail. The cruiser advised us to put a sack under the rope, so as not to injure his skin. And the base-ship's crane lifted him up into the sky. Then he woke up and started to struggle. We hastily cast off and took ourselves out of the way, leaving the sea clear for him. And someone from the base-ship undid the reef knot, and our baby whale plunged into the water, where he dived at once, smacking his tail once on the water with a great splash – and then down, into the depths. And what a 'hurrah' there was from all the ships, hooters sounding and rockets flying up into the sky!

That day was like a holiday. The day itself was so beautiful – blue and sunny. And the baby whale was beautiful. And we were all human beings that day.

There seems to be an echo of the nineteenth-century Russian classics in Vladimov's story: the old yearning for the brotherhood of mankind. Similar echoes can be heard in several stories by Vladimir Tendryakov, who specialises in young people's problems. The main character in his story *The Eclipse*[6] is an idealistic girl named Maya, who reminds one strongly of Turgenev's heroines. Maya is looking for a cause or a person to devote her life to, but she is married to a worthy but dull biologist, Pavel, with whom she feels stifled. She leaves Pavel to live with a red-bearded drop-out named Gosha, who rejects the materialism of Soviet society and goes around preaching brotherly love. From Gosha, Maya learns that just to love one's husband is not enough; one must not be entirely wrapped up in one person, one must spread love all around. 'I love the whole world now,' Maya declares, 'and the world loves me in return.'

Halfway through this story, an incident is described in which Maya's husband Pavel sees a crowd gathered in the street outside a block of flats near his own home. 'They're bringing out the murderer,' someone says, and a couple of militiamen bring out a pale-faced boy in jeans and drive him away in a car. It is a schoolboy of fifteen, who has murdered his drunken father because he was beating up his mother. This crime, presumably drawn from real life, obviously made a great impression on Tendryakov, since he returned to it in a story published two years later, entitled *Retribution*.[7] Here he tries to analyse how such a crime could happen in Soviet society by examining the degree of guilt which ought to rest on every one of the boy-murderer's friends and relatives. As each one of them in turn exclaims 'It's all my fault!' the story takes on a strong tinge of Dostoyevsky. The one who feels most guilty of all is the boy's class-teacher, Arkadi Pamyatnov. He blames himself for having taught his pupils to fight evil actively, to do something about it for themselves and not wait for other people to put things right for them. The result of this teaching, he now feels, is that one of his pupils is a murderer, and that his classmates regard him as a hero. Arkadi also blames a young history-teacher colleague, who told the schoolchildren about the leaders of the *Narodnaya Volya* movement. When he came to the murderer of Tsar Alexander II, Grinevitski, he presented him to the children as a hero: true, he did also tell them that terrorism had not brought about Russia's liberation, but still his pupils learnt from him to admire terrorists. And from this to admiring a present-day murderer was not a long step. Arkadi's conclusion about the murder case, which seems to be endorsed by Tendryakov, is: if the boy Kolya had found more understanding and sympathy from his teachers during the long years when his father was making his home life a misery, this crime would not have happened.

All the stories I have quoted so far centre round young people who in no way question the official moral code. In the late 1970s a much grimmer kind of realism begins breaking into Soviet fiction: the life of the under-privileged is described far more truthfully, and the amoral anti-hero, guided only by self-interest, makes an occasional appearance. Take, for instance, this young man of twenty-two, Nikita Rakhmaninov, from *The Defence*, a story by Zoya Boguslavskaya published in *Novy Mir* in 1978.[8]

Nikita has been in custody for several months, after having beaten up a neighbour, left him for dead in his garage, and then stolen his car. When brought to trial, he admits in court to having told a pack of lies about his crime:

> 'Didn't you realise that it is immoral to tell lies? Do you tell lies all the time?' asked the prosecutor.
>
> 'Yes, if it's necessary. What's so special about that? Lots of people tell lies, and so do I.'
>
> 'But *why*?'
>
> 'Because it makes life much more pleasant. For instance, if you tell a woman you're out of your mind because of her and can't live without her, she feels good and she'll behave more warmly towards you. Whereas if you tell her the truth . . .'

The prosecutor and judge, taken aback by this frank avowal, try to find out more about this young criminal's background. The story quotes an excerpt from the official documents of Nikita's case – a statement he made to his investigator – and it is clear that, like Tendryakov in the last story, Boguslavskaya blames the young criminal's elders for his behaviour. According to Nikita, he had always been spoiled by his parents, who refused him nothing. He grew up without any particular interest in life, and after leaving school he chose the way of life of a 'fixer', mainly because he enjoyed the attention and flattery which is lavished upon anyone who can provide goods or services in short supply. As he told the court, he had plenty of useful connections and could always get hold of things quickly: clothes, a hotel room, batteries for a transistor or film for a cine-camera. At sixteen he learnt to drive his father's car, and from then on he used the car to run errands for people, transporting goods or meeting people at the airport or fetching someone home from hospital. Sometimes he would be paid in kind (the use of a *dacha* for the summer, or an imported jacket), sometimes in cash: but the payment was not the most important thing to him. As he told the court: 'Everywhere people are glad to see me, spoil me and love me . . . I like to be the centre of attention.'

Another young criminal from the same story, Mikhail Tikhonkin, aged seventeen, has confessed to the murder (by repeated stab wounds) of a lad he had never spoken to who had annoyed a member of Tikhonkin's street gang. The victim was chased by the gang and killed in a public park. During the investigation it is established that, although Tikhonkin took the blame as leader of the gang, it was in fact one of the others who did the stabbing. This lad is asked by an investigator: why did you go on stabbing the victim after he had fallen to the ground? 'Because I didn't want the others to think I was sorry for him,' he replies.

Boguslavskaya shows both judges and counsel as horrified at the amoral attitude shown by the young thugs in her story. Her adults ask themselves: where did we go wrong? But they come to no conclusion, and the author herself does not advance any remedy for juvenile hooliganism. One writer who does have such a remedy, albeit a very old-fashioned one, is Veniamin Kaverin, now in his eighties. He recently published two versions of a story about teenagers in a provincial town, entitled *The Puzzle.*[9] The story concerns a three-cornered situation between three sixteen-year olds in the same school class, seen first through the eyes of their teacher, and then through those of a delinquent fellow-pupil. Oleg, the bright son of the local power station boss, who aims to graduate from the Moscow Institute of International Relations and become a Soviet diplomat, has had a long-standing relationship with Nina, the prettiest girl in the class. When these two quarrel briefly, Nina consoles herself with another boy, the talented future artist, Pasha. But the story ends in tragedy: Nina sends an urgent message to Pasha to come and see her, he attempts to swim the local river to reach her side – and is drowned. There is a funeral attended by the whole class – and then the final school year starts, Nina and Oleg make it up, and life goes on with apparently never a thought spared for poor Pasha's memory. The class teacher is horrified at this heartlessness, and wonders: was Pasha just a pawn in a completely cold-blooded game being played by Nina and Oleg? She goes to see an old retired history teacher and asks him what is wrong with today's adolescents. He says they are just waiting for their seniors to tell them about the example of past generations:

> But they are busy from morning to night with their own immediate concerns. The school curriculum is overloaded, it includes a great many subjects, and no one seems aware that there is one very important subject missing, and that's the one I would call 'conscience'. There is in fact one school subject which deals with the concept of conscience, but it is taught very badly. That's our Russian literature, which for the last thousand years has been reminding us of this concept. If literature were to be taught today as it used to be taught in the old *gymnasia*, it could become the basis for discussions with the pupils about conscience, about their moral duty . . .

If Kaverin still seems to think that exhortations about moral values might improve Soviet teenagers' behaviour, other younger writers seem to be taking a gloomier but more realistic view. Some of them are content not to make moral judgements, but to describe with great frankness the physical factors which make many young people's lives a never-ending struggle for existence, and which inevitably push some of them into a life of crime. Nikolai Studenikin, for instance, in 1978 published a story about the grim state of poverty prevailing in many Soviet villages, *Amidst the Tall Corn.*[10] The heroine, Natasha, is a girl factory worker in a provincial town who makes a weekend visit back to her home village to see her family. With her she brings her illegitimate baby, Andrei. It's a long journey by suburban train, then bus, then on foot. Natasha lets the family assume she is married, but in fact her boy-friend abandoned her and she is having a hard time supporting herself and the baby. She goes out to work daily, and has to pay the manageress of the factory hostel where she lives a rouble a day to look after Andrei. Natasha had thought of moving back home to the village with the baby, but soon gives up this idea when she sees the family situation. Her mother and stepfather have just been fined a large sum for brewing *samogon*, or hooch, and selling it at a rouble a half-litre. They explain that one hundred roubles was an unusually big fine, the normal rate being twenty to thirty roubles; but unfortunately they had offended the local militiaman by refusing to sell him the hooch at a cut price.

The whole of Studenikin's story is dominated by lack of money. People travel on the suburban train without a ticket, while a whiskered youth walks up and down the car trying unsuccessfully to flog dirty postcards at two roubles a set. The country bus jolts its way through villages which have shops and street lights – and also wells with wooden pump-handles, from which the women still fetch their water with a wooden yoke and two buckets. Anyone who has travelled in the Soviet countryside is familiar with such scenes; but it is nevertheless surprising that *Novy Mir* was able in 1978 to print a story with such a gloomy picture of Soviet life. None of the characters in this story has time to think about the high ideals that are set before young people during their time in the Soviet educational system: all their energy goes into finding the money for the next meal or the next drink.

Sometimes the suppressed indignation which many young writers seem to feel at the constant indoctrination coming at them from teachers and officials is expressed in the form of gentle satire. An example of this is *The Messenger Boy*, a story by a young Moscow film producer, Karen Shakhnazarov, whose hero is another rebellious teenager, Ivan Miroshnikov.[11] Ivan is seventeen, an idle but gifted lad with lots of imagination but no particular bent in life. After school he fails the entrance examination to a teacher-training college; but his teacher-mother, through a friend, gets him a job as errand-boy on a popular-science magazine. Here he spends his time spinning fantasy-stories to anyone who will listen to him; he particularly likes putting on an act of being an example of all the worst qualities of the younger generation. Thus, when he is sent to deliver a manuscript to one of the magazine's authors, the pompous Professor Kuznetsov, this conversation takes place:

> 'I should like to know, young man, what are the principles on which you propose to conduct your life in society?'
>
> 'They're very simple, no secret about them. I should like to have a good salary, a car, a flat in the centre of town and a small *dacha* on the outskirts, and I should like all this to appear as soon as possible. Oh yes, and one more thing – I should like to work as little as possible. You must agree, work isn't a lot of fun.'

At first the Professor takes this seriously, reads Ivan an indignant lecture, and throws him out of the house. Later he realises it is all fantasising and starts praising Ivan as being an original.

Much more common are stories in which the blame for bad behaviour is transferred from the adolescents to the adults who ought to have looked after them better. This was the moral of Tendryakov's *Retribution*, and it is also the moral of a grim little tale called *The Magnificent Six.*[12] The author is Boris Vasiliev, an older-generation writer who is on the editorial board of the youth magazine, *Yunost.* The setting is a summer Pioneer camp, where six of the senior boys spend their time playing cowboys and Indians. They give each other nicknames like Rocky, Eddie and Dan, and they commandeer some pensioned-off horses they find grazing near the camp and gallop about on them. The horses are old and lame, and on their last evening at the camp the boys reduce them to a state of complete exhaustion. They hitch them to some trees and go back to camp for their supper; and next morning the bus comes to take them home. A week later a militiaman calls at the camp to complain about the boys' treatment of the horses. With him is the old retired groom into whose care the local collective farm had given the animals when they grew too old for work. One of the group-leaders at the camp says yes, some of the boys did go riding. But the woman boss, Kira Sergeyevna, refuses to admit anything. While the militiaman is out of the room, she rounds on her staff: if they confess that it was boys from their camp who went riding without permission, she says, they will have no chance of winning the Pioneer camps competition for the year. Her chief aim in life is not to lose the challenge banner which her camp achieved last year, and out of her zeal, she closes her ears to the militiaman and to the old groom, who is a war invalid and an alcoholic. His main contributions to the conversation are reminiscences about how a horse saved his life in the war, plus requests that someone should give him three roubles and then he will forget the matter of the complaint. The six boys all have outstanding school records, Kira Sergeyevna goes on; they are future mathematicians, linguists, television personalities – 'the hope of the twenty-first century,' she calls them – and their names are not to be blackened by a stupid militiaman and an old drunk. She threatens to report the militiaman to his superiors:

> 'By all means report me,' said the lieutenant. 'And then send someone to bury the corpses of the horses. You'll find them in the wood, on the other side of the ravine.'
>
> A silence fell.
>
> 'You mean – they're dead?' asked the girl group-leader.
>
> 'They died of hunger and thirst,' said the lieutenant. 'When your boys had finished galloping them about, they tied them up to some trees, and then went away leaving them there. The horses ate everything they could reach: leaves, bushes, tree bark. But they were tied up short, so short that even when they died they could not fall to the ground; there they are still, hanging by their bridles.' He took some photographs out of his pocket and laid them on the table. 'Some holidaymakers took these and brought them to me. Now I've brought them to you.'

The lieutenant and the old groom go away, leaving the two women gazing in horror at the photos of the dead horses, their heads pointing up to the sky and their eyes glazed. The boss lady,

Kira Sergeyevna, does shed a tear, but quickly recovers herself, orders the corpses to be buried immediately, and tells one of her staff to find the old groom and give him ten roubles to drink to the memory of his horses – on condition that he keeps his mouth shut. The story ends bleakly:

> When her staff had left the room, Kira Sergeyevna went into her personal washroom, locked herself in, tore up the photographs, threw the fragments into the WC and flushed it, with a feeling of great relief.
>
> But the *kolkhoz* pensioner Pyotr Dementievich Prokudov, formerly a scout in General Belov's cavalry division, died that same evening. He had bought two bottles of vodka, which he consumed in the empty stables where the warm horse smell still lingered on.

That tale of youthful hooligans being allowed to shed all responsibility for their actions is paralleled in much recent fiction about adults, where a purity campaign is being waged against bribery, anonymous denunciations and hushing-up operations of all kinds.

REFERENCES

1 Elena Rzhevskaya, *Zemnoye prityazhenie* (*Novy Mir* 1962, no. 6).

2 Viktoria Tokareva, *Den' bez vraniya* (*Molodaya Gvardiya* 1964, no. 7).

3 Vasili Aksyonov, *Zvyozdnyi bilet* (*Yunost* 1961, no. 6).

4 Vasili Aksyonov, *Na polputi k lune* (*Novy Mir* 1962, no. 7).

5 Georgi Vladimov, *Tri minuty molchaniya* (*Novy Mir* 1969, nos. 7–9).

6 Vladimir Tendryakov, *Zatmenie* (*Druzhba Narodov* 1977, no. 5).

7 Vladimir Tendryakov, *Rasplata* (*Novy Mir* 1979, no. 3).

8 Zoya Boguslavskaya, *Zashchita* (*Novy Mir* 1978, no. 10).

9 Veniamin Kaverin, *Zagadka* (*Oktyabr* 1984, no. 1 & 1985, no. 1).

10 Nikolai Studenikin, *Mezh vysokikh khlebov* (*Novy Mir* 1978, no. 7).

11 Karen Shakhnazarov, *Kurier* (*Yunost* 1982, no. 4).

12 Boris Vasiliev, *Velikolepnaya shestyorka* (*Yunost* 1980, no. 6).

3 Criminals and Fixers

A standard situation which crops up time after time in Soviet officially-published fiction is the one where an unscrupulous professional man wants to blacken a rival's character. Sometimes he does so by having recourse to anonymous letters. An example occurs in a play published in *Moskva.*[1] The villain of the piece, a junior surgeon who is intriguing for the downfall of the head of his clinic, asks a favour of his mistress – one of the nurses:

> 'Surely you could find me some women who for three roubles or so would each write an anonymous letter? Aren't there any such women around?'
>
> 'Of course there are. But they won't do it for three roubles. The rate for anonymous letters has gone up. They'll want five roubles this time.'

That bit of dialogue comes from a play by Anatoli Sofronov, one of the best-known Soviet playwrights, an establishment man through and through, author of countless heavily-promoted patriotic songs and editor of the magazine *Ogonyok* for more than twenty-five years. A casual reference to anonymous letter-writing from such a writer seems to indicate both that the practice is a very common phenomenon of Soviet life, and that it is one which the authorities would now like to see abolished. Indeed, a few months after Sofronov's play appeared, Leonid Brezhnev in addressing the XXVI Party Congress roundly condemned the anonymous slanderers. He was urging Party members to pay more attention to letters and suggestions from ordinary Soviet citizens. But then he added:

I am referring to letters that are sincere and honest. As regards all sorts of anonymous vilifications the Party stand is well known: there should be no room for them in our life. Those who come forward with well-founded, businesslike criticisms do not have to hide their faces.

Old habits, however, die hard: Brezhnev was speaking in February 1981, and in November of the same year the factory-boss hero of a play by the Belorussian writer Alexander Petrashkevich was complaining that such a campaign of anonymous letters had been mounted against him that in the course of the last four months he had been investigated by six separate commissions, all wanting to discover if it was true that he had been poaching deer, drinking too much, or sleeping with his secretary. In the end he was able to prove that all the letters had been written on the same typewriter, belonging to one of his enemies.

Official discouragement of anonymous slanders ties in with several recently published stories where any attempt to avoid responsibility for one's actions, or to hush up an accidental crime, is strongly condemned. One particularly damning account of a successful cover-up occurs in a story by a writer of the older generation, Yuri Nagibin, entitled *An Incident on the Road.*[2] Two professional couples – Leningrad architect Kirill with his wife Zhanna, and Moscow scientist Igor with his wife Olga – are returning home by car from a joint holiday spent looking at old monasteries to the north of Moscow. They are coming down a main road, with Zhanna driving – and at the same time flirting with Olga's husband Igor, who is sitting beside her in front:

> Zhanna saw the old man in plenty of time, coming straight out like an idiot on to the main road with his moped, and she hooted at him. The old fool should have turned on to the hard shoulder, but what Zhanna did not know was that he was deaf and never heard the horn. She glanced at the speedometer which read 60 km per hour – a perfectly legal speed. She clicked her cigarette-lighter and was about to say something to Igor, when she suddenly noticed his grimace, his wide-open mouth shouting 'Stop!' She braked sharply, and immediately felt the car hit something; she was thrown forward against the steering wheel . . .

The old man does not seem much damaged, although his moped is a write-off, and a couple of men from the nearby village appear and take charge of him. Olga wants to take him to hospital, but the other three are concerned to get away as quickly as possible. The car is luckily undamaged, the old man was far too dazed to take a note of the registration number, and thus they can evade all responsibility for the accident. Olga continues to protest, but is overruled by her husband and friends, who give the incident no further thought . . . Olga broods about it, however, and some months later she takes a bus out of Moscow, back to the scene of the unreported crime. She walks into the nearby village and asks for the old man who used to ride a moped, pretending that he was letting part of his house to her for the summer. He's dead, an old woman tells her: he seemed to get over the accident, but then one day, sitting quietly in his house mending a jacket, he suddenly fell down dead. Olga goes home, has a row with her husband which ends in fisticuffs – and is left to carry her burden of remorse alone.

With the increasing traffic on Soviet roads, many more such hit-and-run incidents must be happening in real life – especially as, under Soviet law, a driver who is held responsible for a road accident may have to pay compensation to the victim for the rest of his life. This powerful motive for hushing up an accident is also present in a longer and more ambitious story by Yuri Geiko, which appeared in *Novy Mir.*[3] The setting is a small settlement for oil-drillers and prospectors out in the Kazakhstan steppe. The hero, Sasha Ageyev, takes a temporary job here as a lorry-driver in the hope of making a fast rouble; he has just finished his army service in the Soviet Far East and is on his way to his widowed mother near Moscow.

The story opens with a masterly description – very laconic, with none of the long-windedness which is the curse of so much Soviet fiction – of Sasha waking up in the oilmen's hostel, where he shares a room with his mate, Kolya Kvasiuk. The washbasin tap is making a gurgling noise, it is hot and dusty, and a bed-bug is crawling up his leg. On the wall opposite him he can see Kolya's collection of pin-ups: the Soviet girls all have their clothes on, the foreign girls do not. From the next-door rooms come the sounds of alarm-clocks going off and people getting up. It's his day off, and Sasha wonders: why isn't he glad that the sun is shining and a new day stretches before him, a long day with no more army discipline? Yuri Geiko has set the scene: we already know this is going to be a story about young people and frustration. Kolya seems happy to earn good money and spend it on drink and girls, but Sasha wants more – he wants a purpose to devote his life to. He is a good mechanic, enjoys driving his lorry and tinkering with its engine; but there is nothing to do in his spare time except join Kolya in his amorous exploits – and the girl Kolya finds for him, Ira, is very plain. There is a workers' club, but it is dominated by a gang of young thugs just out of prison, who wear imported jeans suits and amuse themselves by beating up newcomers. So when his boss, Mikhail Pochka, arranges for him to go hunting with a couple of other lads on his free day, Sasha happily agrees. But he finds he is involved in an enterprise that is both illegal and highly dangerous. They go out with a lorry at night, hunting the small antelopes – *saigak* – which are a protected species. One man drives the lorry, the others stand in the back with rifles. The corpses of the deer are loaded into the lorry and taken home to be sold to the local bosses for a good price. At first Sasha has doubts about this kind of hunting, but he soon loses them when a big herd of *saigak* appears, and in the excitement of the chase blood-lust takes over:

> Afterwards I could remember little about the next period of time that ensued: it was measured not by minutes but by three dozen cartridges, and all I recall is the beasts' backs, their legs kicking in the air, their bodies somersaulting in the dust . . .

After a while, it is Sasha's turn to drive, and his two companions, one of whom is his best friend Kolya, stand in the back of the lorry. Carried away with enthusiasm, Sasha drives like a madman after the herd, twisting the wheel right or left as he singles out the biggest beasts for his friends to pick off. But he turns the wheel too sharply and Kolya falls out while the lorry is doing over a hundred kilometres an hour: his back is broken, and he has head injuries as well. They drive him back to the settlement, and he is flown out by helicopter to hospital in the town of Karaganda.

Now comes the cover-up operation: Kolya's boss, Pochka, rigs up a phony accident scene out in the steppe, where they dig a hole in the sand and drive the lorry over it, dropping Kolya's lighter and packet of cigarettes nearby. All traces of blood from the deer carcasses are removed from the lorry and from their clothing, and the story for the police investigator is that while they were driving out to an oil-drill on the boss's orders, Kolya Kvasiuk fell out of the back of the lorry – purely from his own carelessness, losing his balance while lighting a cigarette. The investigator accepts this version of what happened, and the case is closed without going to court.

The story might have ended here: but Yuri Geiko evidently wanted to make sure that his readers joined him in condemnation of Sasha's lack of moral fibre. He only took part in the hunting expedition because he was too weak to dissociate himself from the majority; and now he goes along with the cover-up operation because, again, he is too weak to stand up and tell the truth about what happened. The next pages of the story are set in Karaganda, where Kolya lies in hospital, almost certainly paralysed for life. His simple peasant mother watches by his bedside, and he is clearly going to be a burden to her for many years to come. One day the man in the next bed, also a paraplegic, explains the legal situation to the mother and son. Whoever was driving the lorry, he tells them, ought to be held legally responsible for the accident, and a court should compel him to pay compensation – probably twenty-five per cent of his earnings.

Sasha's boss is well aware of this law. When Sasha goes by train to Karaganda to see Kolya in hospital, Pochka drives him to the station and gives him an envelope containing money. 'Give this to Kvasiuk's mother,' he says, 'and see there are no witnesses when you hand it over. If they take the money, that's the end of the matter.' Again Sasha does as he is told, adding some money of his own. Later on, the man in the next bed sees Kolya's mother with the money and helps her count it.

> 'There's two hundred ten-rouble notes here, Hanna Davydovna – that's two thousand roubles.'
>
> 'Two thousand . . . Why so much? Whatever for?'
>
> 'Because the whole business stinks, in my opinion. It wasn't Nikolai's fault that he got hurt. This is blood money.'
>
> 'Is it all right to take the money, do you think?'
>
> 'Of course you can take it, but there isn't as much here as there ought to be.'

'Not as much . . .?'

'Work it out for yourself: that driver gets 400 roubles or more a month, doesn't he? Right then. Twenty-five per cent of that's a bit over a hundred – nearly 1500 roubles a year. It won't matter if your Nikolai gets well again, then he won't need any money, but supposing he ends up like me – then what are you going to feed him on? This money they've given you, it's only peanuts compared with what ought to be due to you from the person responsible for the accident. That's what I mean.'

Kolya listens to the conversation. The accident *was* Sasha's fault, he thinks: he should never have turned the wheel so sharply. But what good would it do to send Sasha to prison or fine him – what punishment could recompense him, Kolya, for his present state of living death? He tells his mother: take the money.

But Sasha can't forget what has happened to his friend. All through the story, Geiko shows his hero consumed with moral doubts: he asks himself – was it right to kill the *saigak* deer? If they had had hunters' licences, would that have given them any more moral right to kill? And what was the act of killing doing to them, the hunters? Was it debasing them? He suspects that it was, and he is sure that a couple of thousand roubles are not going to dispose of the guilt he feels about the deer and about the accident. He goes back to his girl-friend Ira and says – what should I do? He would like to go to the prosecutor's office and tell them what really happened: but he is worried about how his mother and sister back home would manage if he were to get a prison sentence. Ira tells him he must make a choice: either to do what he wants to do and be strong, or not do it and be like everyone else he knows, too weak to stand up for their principles. And Yuri Geiko's story ends with Sasha finally growing up. He goes off early next morning – the story ends as it began, with the hero waking up – but this time he takes a decision, leaves Ira still sleeping, and goes out to accept the responsibility for his actions.

Geiko's story had an unusual setting in the Kazakhstan steppes; there are far more stories in the literary journals about town life. One which gives a very frank account of inefficiency and corruption in Soviet industry is *The Peddlers* by A. Kashtanov, which appeared in *Novy Mir* a few months after Geiko's story.[4] Once again the hero is an honest man, but he finds himself trapped in a situation where he cannot do his job properly without breaking the law. An engineer named Yushkov, he gets a job in the supply department of a big car factory. As his first assignment, he is sent on a duty trip to a metallurgical combine, to hurry up delivery of the ten wagonloads of high-quality steel which this combine has undertaken to supply to his factory. Yushkov is given a travel allowance and a special extra cash grant, and told to go to the factory's closed shop, where the assistant sells him powdered coffee, sausage and chocolates to take with him on the trip. When he arrives at his destination, he finds the hotel full of other factory representatives, some of whom spend a couple of months here every year trying to wangle steel shipments. In the hotel restaurant he shares a table with a man from Nizhny Tagil in the Urals, who tells him he will never get his steel unless he has something valuable to offer in exchange:

> 'Peddlers, that's what we all are.'
>
> 'Why peddlers?'
>
> 'You don't know your history. There used to be people in the old days called peddlers, who went round supplying the needs of the population.'

Later Yushkov asks one of the other works representatives hanging about at the hotel how the man from Nizhny Tagil had managed to get his wagonload of steel. For him it's easy, comes the answer: he's got an order with him, entitling him to some electrical motors in short supply; he gives them the motors, they give him the steel. Now Yushkov gets the message. He finds a key girl in the steel-mill orders office and bribes her with chocolates and coffee powder. He wires his mother to send him some pots of face-cream which he gives to the hotel manageress, who has some influence with the steel-mill bosses. Then he makes friends with the smelters, finds out when the next lot of steel will be ready, gets six wagonloads and returns home triumphant.

Kashtanov's hero now has an excellent grasp of the barter principle on which Soviet industry seems to work. Five years on, after several more successful trips to butter up the car factory's suppliers, Yushkov gets promoted. Now he is assistant head of the supply department, and has to deal with visiting 'peddlers' from other factories who want car spares and who now try to bribe him as he used to bribe the steelworkers. Then his boss, Belan, is suddenly arrested on charges of speculation and taking bribes, and investigators arrive and ask a lot of questions. Why, for instance, they ask, did Belan give representatives from the supply department large cash grants before sending them out to see the suppliers? Yushkov tries to explain the system: this is the only way the factory can operate, he says. The suppliers don't fulfil their obligations to the car works, which never gets all the raw materials in time to fulfil its annual plan. If the factory took the suppliers to court, it could get them fined for their failure to deliver: but that would destroy any existing goodwill and would mean more trouble the following year. Something is always in short supply: yesterday headlamps, today washers. The factory has to send out its representatives to obtain these essential goods, and has to pay them overtime. In other words, small rules have to be broken in order to comply with production quotas.

The rules, however, are all that interest the investigators, and they refuse to listen to Yushkov. Then they begin to press him as to whether he has not only been handing out bribes, but accepting them too. Just before his boss Belan was arrested, he had told Yushkov to issue two car engines to a representative from a Ukrainian factory, and to collect from this man a debt of 300 roubles which he allegedly owed to Belan. Surely, the investigator asks, Yushkov must have suspected that this money was a bribe? Yushkov has to admit that, yes, he did suspect bribery when he spotted the rouble notes tucked in between the official papers which the Ukrainian representative handed to him. According to the investigator's strict code of morals, he should have protested at once instead of quietly taking the money and passing it on to his obviously corrupt boss. Yushkov tries again to explain that life in the car industry is not all black or white, and cannot always be lived according to the rules. But he gets no sympathy from the investigator:

> 'You seriously think I ought to have got mad at him?' Yushkov said.
>
> 'Didn't it make you angry?' Pozdeyev enquired.

'Of course not.'

'That's an interesting admission.'

'Look here,' said Yushkov, 'you're wearing a sham-leather jacket. Where did you get it from?'

'Let's just finish this conversation first, and then we'll talk about my jacket.'

'They aren't on sale in the shops; they're in short supply. You can only get them through acquaintances. Doesn't that worry you? Perhaps someone gave it to you. In that case, somebody else got hold of it through an acquaintance. Does that make you angry? No, I can see it doesn't. . . . For over five years I have been giving useful people chocolates or plying them with vodka. And after all that, you think I ought to have got mad over those 300 roubles? If that's so, I ought to have gone out of my mind long, long ago.'

Yushkov escapes a prison sentence; his boss Belan confesses to taking bribes and gets ten years. Yushkov is left in a very unenviable situation, in Belan's old job. However much he tries to obey the rules, he can see that he is never going to achieve fulfilment of the car factory's annual plan without greasing a lot of palms along the way. Belan has been made an example of: probably Yushkov will be the next. The only time Kashtanov's unfortunate hero is described as having a good laugh – if rather a sour one – is when he visits a friend in hospital, and finds the same investigator, Pozdeyev, is also a patient there. Yushkov catches the investigator giving the woman doctor boxes of sweets to ensure preferential treatment for himself.

This situation – the hero who wants to be honest and keep to the rules, but who is never able to avoid breaking them – has been cropping up more and more often in Soviet literature. In autumn 1981, for instance, *Oktyabr* published a story by Svyatoslav Rybas called *On Wheels*,[5] which told of the tribulations of the head of a big car-service centre not far from Moscow. When first opened a few years before, this centre earned itself a reputation for excellent service to all comers, without any bribes or special favours. But gradually the workers got corrupted by the customers, and now the boss, Nikiforov, can't stop the rot spreading. When he catches the mechanics accepting money, he makes them sign confessions which he keeps on a file in his office. Here is one of them:

> I, V.M. Molokanov, was called to inspect a car coming in for repairs. I was asked to give an opinion on the nearside bumper and wing. After examination, I said the bumper could be straightened out, but a new wing would be required. As I was about to return to the workshop the customer stopped me and slipped fifty roubles into my pocket. I refused to take the money, but he said it was payment for the opinion I had given. I said – I don't take money before the work is done. But he put the notes back in my pocket again, and this time I did not protest, but went back to the workshop. I acknowledge my guilt, and promise that such a thing will not occur again.

But of course it does, and there is no way Nikiforov can stop it. He has a problem with his storekeeper, whom he authorises to give presents of Courvoisier brandy to representatives from the car components factories, but who one day is found to have drawn a windscreen from the store for his own use. He has a lot of trouble with an old schoolfellow, now an inspector in the highway patrol service: he wants a new roof for a relative's car, and when Nikiforov tells him he can't jump the queue but must wait till the next lot of supplies comes in, the inspector begins harassing him. He stops Nikiforov's car as he drives home from work, and insists on taking him to the local hospital to be tested for drunken driving. There is more trouble with a man from the State Bank, who complains that repairs to his official car were grossly overcharged. Nikiforov gets the bill reduced; but as he explains wearily, overcharging is bound to happen under a system where the mechanics receive one-quarter of all the charges made for the repairs they carry out. With such incentives to dishonesty, how can any boss enforce honest behaviour from his workers?

Another sphere of Soviet life where corruption has been notoriously rife for many years is the retail trade. There are plenty of fictional examples of shop assistants or managers who are venal, inefficient or simply idle, to the fury of the customers. Just recently there has been an official campaign to raise the standards and the social status of the service industries, and this has resulted in at least one attempt by a novelist to depict an honest, energetic store manager. In *The Department Store*[6] Ilya Shtemler takes as his hero Konstantin Firtich, the director of the big 'Olympus' store in a provincial town. Firtich wants to reorganise the store and introduce Western trading methods – he installs closed-circuit television, tells his shop assistants that the customers are always right, and does his best to serve public demand. He believes in getting rid of unsatisfactory lines rather than letting goods pile up in the warehouses, and he disagrees with colleagues who do not approve of holding seasonal sales. He is negotiating with two foreign firms (Scandinavian and American) who are competing for the contract to convert his building to a complex departmental system, where there will be show kitchens, bathrooms, etc. – the components of which can all be ordered and delivered to the customer's home. But Firtich is frustrated by the Soviet system of rigid monthly trading quotas, and by the unwillingness of his bosses to allow him freedom of decision. Moreover, he is hampered at every turn by the blatant dishonesty of some of his employees and all of his colleagues, his fellow shop managers (most of whom have served prison sentences).

These dishonest managers are engaged in all the tricks which writers in Soviet newspapers denounce from time to time: bribes are handed over, books are fiddled, goods leave the warehouses but never reach the shops, and so on. Even in Firtich's store the department managers tolerate the operations of a woman speculator, 'Signora' Svetlana Belskaya, whose routine is described in some detail in the novel. Blonde Svetlana, dressed from top to toe in foreign imported clothes, is always in the front of the crowd which waits outside for the 'Olympus' to open each morning. She is always first through the doors and, thanks to inside information, is able to go straight to whichever department is selling scarce goods that day. Then she makes regular rounds with her purchases, visiting clients in various parts of town:

> For instance, in the three-storeyed brick building housing the Building and Installation Administration. Many of the workers there have Svetlana's visiting days marked off in red in their office calendars. She usually appears on the first and third Mondays of the month. The doorman never asks to see her

> pass, he knows her face, and even carries her bag in for her. She is able to trade quite openly – except sometimes towards the end of the month, when things hot up and overseers are continually coming through the offices. Then she transfers her trading to the cloakroom, where there's plenty of room and no need to hide behind a filing cabinet or wedge the door shut with a chair-leg before trying some garment on . . .

The novel ends irresolutely: we are given no indication as to whether Firtich will succeed in revolutionising Soviet trading methods, or whether he will be called to account for allowing his monthly turnover to drop.

Shtemler's novel was published in *Novy Mir* in 1982, by which time the official battle against corruption had been launched and the Soviet reading public (with whom the novel is said to be very popular) were ready to sympathise with a manager trying to do his job honestly. Five years earlier, a novel published in the same journal, *Insomnia* by Alexander Kron,[7] described a blatant case of bribery in a Moscow food store, without any suggestion that anyone was going to do something about it. The storyteller in this novel is a biologist who is a regular customer at the shop on the ground floor of his block of flats. He finds that the salesgirls are regularly overcharging the customers, and after arguing with one of them he goes to see the manager, to register a complaint. He is shown into a large office, where he gets a very cool reception from the manager, a young man named Shalashov, wearing a smart imported suit and with his hair carefully set:

> . . . Two minutes passed . . . Shalashov gave a slight nod of the head. He put out a hand towards the turnover calendar on his desk and tore off a pale blue sheet of paper. He thought for a moment, and then turned an unseeing glance upon me.
>
> 'Do you want some canned roach?'
>
> I did not understand the question at first. Then I realised what he had meant, and hastened to explain the purpose of my visit. Shalashov listened without interruption, fiddling with his Parker pen with its big nail-like gold nib. His face expressed absolutely nothing: it was neither sympathetic nor hostile.
>
> 'We shall take your criticisms into consideration,' he said at

length . . . 'So you don't want any roach? All right, I'll give you some crabmeat.'

Kron's hero leaves the manager's office in a rage, protesting that he does not want anything. But the manager gets his secretary to make up a box of goodies which never see the open shelves of his food shop: caviare, smoked salmon, tins of crabmeat and instant coffee, and a dozen oranges – and the package is delivered later in the day to the hero's flat, by the house manager.

Kron describes that bribery scene with more humour than indignation, and shows his hero as forced into the attitude of resigned acceptance which most Soviet town-dwellers adopt towards such goings-on. In the last few years, however, attitudes towards crime have hardened, and the anti-corruption campaign has been intensified in the press, first under Andropov and now under Gorbachev. The first realistic reflection of this campaign in fiction came six months before Brezhnev's death, when *Moskva* published a novel by Lazar Karelin, *The Snake Catcher.*[8] This was clearly based on the 'caviare scandal', which rumbled on for three years and culminated in the execution of the former Deputy Minister of the Fishing Industry, Rytov, which was announced in April 1982, the month the novel appeared.

Karelin's hero, Pavel Shorokhov, is the former manager of a big food store, who has just done a five-year term in camp and exile for various malpractices. He was released early from prison for good conduct, and then spent a year in the Kara-Kala desert working at a serpentarium, catching snakes to make money (he got thirty roubles per cobra, but had to keep cutting pieces off himself whenever they bit him). He comes back to Moscow and is at once plunged into the world of venomous human snakes. Kotov, the head of the criminal gang for whom he took the rap, is dying of cancer and his henchmen are preparing for the succession struggle. On his deathbed, Kotov gives Shorokhov his coded notebook, containing diagrams of the distribution system for illegally obtained goods. The personalities involved are designated by initials, and all the fish deals come under the letter R (Rytov) but marked with a cross – indicating that the 'R' has now been liquidated.

The novel contains a splendid description of the funeral of the underworld boss, Pyotr Kotov. The coffin travels to the cemetery in a bus which is followed by a cortège of mourners in brand-new small Zhiguli cars. These are Kotov's men: trading bosses from small foodshops, who have plenty of money but who know their place. They don't aspire to run Volgas, but instead buy a Zhiguli and fit it out with powerful headlamps, radio aerials, sun shields, dangling mascots and so on. At the *pominki* or wake, held in the dead man's flat, his passing is celebrated in great style:

> The table was groaning with food. You could tell by the magnificence of the spread how high the social standing of the departed had been. Everything that was in short supply in Moscow – smoked eels in the middle of summer, pale pink salmon, sterlet that only yesterday or the day before were still swimming around in the upper reaches of the Kama river, huge crayfish from the Caspian, pink shrimps from the Far East, golden smoked fish from the Baltic – it was all there, all the unobtainable types of fish, here on this table, the products of rivers, seas and oceans . . . A spread like this would have satisfied even that most hospitable of men, Lefort, when he was entertaining his friend Tsar Peter. And how were the guests seated around the main table? In much the same order as in the days of the young Tsar Peter, when the boyars were still powerful and when they pushed and shoved to get themselves a place of honour on the bench, as near as possible to the Tsar. At the head of the table, next to Tamara Ivanovna and Sasha [the widow and son], sat fat Mitrich; and to their right and left, in strict accordance with some invisible order which was clearly obvious to them, sat solid, thick-set men, all of them wielding authority in their own spheres within commercial Moscow.

Mitrich, who had been Kotov's chief henchman although Kotov had not trusted him, proposes the first toast to the deceased: 'Peter the Great!' Later in the evening, when they are all getting drunk, he proposes another toast to which they all clink glasses – to goods in short supply (*defitsit*):

> 'We're all friends here, so I'll admit: *defitsit* is the field where we have a great pull. Stealing from the State? Good heavens,

no, we wouldn't do that. But if something is in short supply, and you know how to get hold of it, to do someone a favour – then where's the harm in that?'

Karelin's novel ends on an optimistic note: the hero, Pavel Shorokhov, survives a knife attack by two hired assassins from the underworld, and he passes Kotov's notebook to the police, who presumably will round up the criminal network.

The story stops short before the round-up begins; Soviet literature has not yet created a convincing policeman hero. An attempt to do this, in a story published in the Leningrad journal *Neva*, was so inept as to be unintentionally extremely funny. Called *Major Orlov's Duty Day*,[9] the story centres on Major Yuri Orlov, a Leningrad cop with a heart of gold. Orlov is a father-figure to lonely old ladies and unhappy animals in his district. He is a widower with a problem adopted teenager son; and his utter devotion to his work is ruining his love-life. He queues up to buy sweets to feed to the police dogs; and in seventeen years of service with the militia he has only fired a gun once, and then in the air. In the course of one twenty-four-hour duty spell he manages to nail one burglar and sort out some gipsies caught selling sweets without a licence. But his greatest achievement is to find a missing pregnant Siamese cat and take it back to its elderly owner. One fears that he would be no match for Mitrich and his merry men.

Far more typical are the stories, some of which I have cited above, of industrial managers or shop directors who spend their lives struggling to make an impossible system work, with all the odds against them and facing the strong probability that they will end up in jail. The best-known (and best-written) story of this kind, about a building-site foreman, is *I'd Like to be Honest* by Vladimir Voinovich, which came out in *Novy Mir* twenty years ago.[10] The hero, Samokhin, is foreman on a building site, a man without any ambition who chose this line of work quite by accident and is not enjoying himself in it. He fights a losing battle against slipshod workmanship on the part of his employees and indifference on the part of his bosses. While struggling to finish a block of flats on time despite continual shortages of vital materials, he is asked to sign the document certifying the new building as fit for habitation, and promised promotion if he signs. Samokhin knows that the new flats are very far from ready, and he takes a stand on principle. Through all the frustration and unpleasant conflicts of work which he does not like, he has been sustained until now by the consciousness that he is at least doing an honest job. Now the bosses are taking this last consolation from him, and Samokhin rebels. He reflects to himself:

> 'Whatever comes of it, I won't sign this document. Whether my work is good or bad, it's all I've got. And if I start not doing this work as I want to – to my best capacity – then what's the point of any of my life?'

And to a foreman colleague who asks why he is being so obstinate, he says:

> 'I wasn't being clever. I simply don't want to cheat on the job. I want to be honest.'
>
> 'But who wants your honesty?'
>
> '*I* want it.'
>
> 'You're a blockhead. You could have been a chief engineer by now.'
>
> 'I'll manage without promotion.'
>
> 'You'll be a senior foreman all your life – if they don't demote you.'
>
> 'And do you reckon that happiness is – the rank you hold?'
>
> 'Well, if it isn't that, then where do you think happiness is?'
>
> 'I don't know: maybe it's the rank, maybe not. But at least I know I'm living the way I want to live. I'm not trying to outsmart anyone, I'm not sucking up to anyone, I'm not frightened of losing the job I have . . . I can always go to work in Siberia . . .'

Samokhin gets no promotion: instead he gets a heart attack – but he keeps his self-respect. Voinovich's story was published in 1963, and it is interesting to compare it with a more modern story with the same basic plot. This is *Repentance*[11] by Alexander Astrakhantsev, which came out in 1981. Once again the hero works on a building site, this time as a boss and not a foreman. But like Samokhin, he cannot get the planned work quotas completed on time unless he not only overlooks poor workmanship, but even bribes the workmen with money or vodka. He falls under the evil influence of one of his works foremen, who shows him how to get the necessary money by constructing a whole system of Gogolesque 'dead souls'. Non-existent labourers are put on the books, imaginary work-sheets are written out for them, their salaries are drawn by their bosses and used partly to line their own pockets and partly for extra money, cognac and vodka given to vital workers, or to pay for drinking–fishing parties arranged for the entertainment of higher bosses. When the day of reckoning comes the site boss gets five years in jail and the foreman three. But the clear winner in this story is the foreman, whose favourite motto is the exact reverse of that of Voinovich's hero: 'Heroism means living just one day honestly. But we aren't heroes!'

REFERENCES

1 Anatoli Sofronov, *Operatsiya na serdtse* (*Moskva* 1981, no. 8).
2 Yuri Nagibin, *Dorozhnoye proisshestvie* (*Oktyabr* 1980, no. 11).
3 Yuri Geiko, *Saiga* (*Novy Mir* 1980, no. 10).
4 A. Kashtanov, *Korobeiniki* (*Novy Mir* 1981, nos. 6–7).
5 Svyatoslav Rybas, *Na kolyosakh* (*Oktyabr* 1981, no. 10).
6 Ilya Shtemler, *Univermag* (*Novy Mir* 1982, nos. 8–10).
7 Alexander Kron, *Bessonitsa* (*Novy Mir* 1977, nos. 4–6).
8 Lazar Karelin, *Zmeyelov* (*Moskva* 1982, no. 4).
9 M. Glinka, *Khronika dezhurstva Maiora Orlova* (*Neva* 1982, no. 12).
10 Vladimir Voinovich, *Khochu byt' chestnym* (*Novy Mir* 1963, no. 2).
11 Alexander Astrakhantsev, *Raskayanie* (*Nash Sovremennik* 1981, no. 9).

4 Changes in the Countryside

Country themes have always figured largely in Russian literature, and rural life provided the inspiration for many of the nineteenth-century classic writers. Turgenev, Tolstoy, Chekhov all gave us plenty of lyrical descriptions of the countryside and portraits of a wide range of rural types from patriarchs to beggars. The Revolution caused a temporary break in this tradition: no one could publish the truth about what famine and collectivisation were doing to the countryside in the 1920s and 1930s, and most writers concentrated instead on the heroes of industrialisation. In the Stalinist years peasants began creeping back into Soviet fiction, but usually as quaint survivals from an outmoded way of life, due for improvement and modernisation. Then there was a period after the war when stereotyped stories of country life would appear: the hero was usually the honest *kolkhoz* chairman, who knew what was best for his land and his workers, but who got pushed around continually by ignorant townee Party officials. But gradually touches of real life began breaking through to enliven these stories, and in the 1960s and 1970s a whole school of 'country writers' (*derevenshchiki*) emerged. They are the pride of official Soviet literature at the moment – and oddly enough are also greatly admired by émigré writers such as Solzhenitsyn. Some of these authors write extremely good prose, while others are repetitive and tedious: but a new feature common to all of them is their surprisingly truthful descriptions of the changes that have been taking place on Soviet farms since the war.

One of the best-known writers of the 'country' school is Vasili Belov, who himself started life as a *kolkhoz* worker in the northern Vologda district. One of his first stories, *The Scrounger*, published in *Novy Mir* in 1968, was about life in remote rural Russia in the last winter of the war.[1] The scrounger is Senya Gruzdev, who was wounded at the front early in the war, went back to his northern village in 1942 with only one arm, and since then has been begging or stealing right and left to feed his wife and five children. The *kolkhoz* sends him off on regular journeys, taking loads of flax to the mill in the nearest town. This usually means leading a convoy of four sledges, driven by himself, two women and a fifteen-year-old boy. Belov describes Gruzdev going out early on one of these mornings to the stable to harness the old roan gelding, Sparrow. Having only one hand, Gruzdev uses his teeth to undo the bridle straps, and it is so cold that when his lips touch the metal bit he gets frost-burn:

> Usually it was already light by the time they were ready to set out. There would be a pink light in the sky, and here and there the chimney smoke, going straight up. The horses would immediately start to go grey as the frost formed on them, and the sledge-runners would begin their melancholy squeaking song. Now at least three days' journey lay ahead of them, with nothing to do but listen to that squeaking through the frost. Sparrow would stop from time to time on the outskirts of a village, as though asking, 'Maybe you made a mistake – maybe we're not going far after all, this time?' Gruzdev could see the question in the horse's eye as he looked back at his driver. No, no mistake – 'Get up there!' he shouted at Sparrow, huddling deeper into his sheepskin coat. The cold sun came up over the pink, almost bloodstained snow. Everywhere there was a dead silence, the alder bushes white with frost. It was seventy kilometres to the railway station.

They have to stop over a couple of nights on the way, and Gruzdev successfully buys food for himself and the other drivers and steals some hay for the horses. After delivering their loads at the flax mill, they are all hungry again and have only a few kopecks between them. Gruzdev takes them into a café and tries a very old trick: he orders one tea and one soup, then drops some dead flies in the soup and makes such a fuss about the lack of hygiene that the waitress brings them fresh bowlfuls all round, free of charge.

This was the only way Gruzdev knew to make sure they started the three-day journey home with some hot food inside them.

That story, set in the winter of 1944–5, has had several successors revealing the truth about hunger in the villages in the immediate post-war years. A recent example is an autobiographical tale by a Chuvash writer, Dmitri Mikhleyev.[2] Born in 1942 in a Volga village, he recalls his hungry childhood in the days when wolves would attack children and horses in winter, and when the old grannies would pray to the heathen Chuvash gods to send the longed-for rain in summer:

> When the war ended, new troubles came: two bad harvests, droughts when everything dried up. People could no longer survive thanks to their allotments; they ran off to the towns, and the *kolkhozy* emptied. For a labour-day they used to pay out half a glassful of flour and 100 grams of rye. The grannies hid the flour in locked trunks, because we children soon found out what it tasted like, and would eat it by the handful if we got the chance. Coughing and covered in flour dust, we would take it to the river and mix it up with spring water in a pot of some kind – it made a good drink, tasty and satisfying. It was a lot better than eating mud, which we also did – not the red mud, but the grey-green kind which was soft and fatty (or so we thought), and which we scooped out from under the banks of the pond. We would make little figures out of it and then suck them, like the modern children who suck those clay cocks bought in the market. Then we would get stomach pains – but we went on eating the mud. The women learnt how to make soup out of sorrel and cakes out of various forest plants. Plenty of old people and children died in those two years, and so did many of the cripples who came home from the war. Two of my sisters, fourteen and sixteen years old, died – that's what it was like at that time for people in the Volga area . . .

Slowly, over the post-war years, things have been improving on Soviet farms. The main chronicler of these changes, and of the changing mood of the Soviet peasantry, has been the novelist Fyodor Abramov, who died in 1983. Brought up himself in a peasant family in the Archangel district, Abramov wrote a series of four novels, for which he got a State prize, about the fortunes of a family like his own, the Pryaslins, in the years from 1942 up to the present day. The first of these novels, published in 1958, was called *Brothers and Sisters*.[3] It dealt with the hard wartime years in a remote village in northern Russia. The local *kolkhoz* chairman goes off to the army, as do all the other able-bodied men, and the chairman's wife is left to run the collective farm with only women and one fifteen-year-old boy – the hero, Mikhail Pryaslin. Mikhail's father is killed at the front, and from then on he has six dependants to support – his mother, two younger sisters and three brothers. The novel was greatly praised and made Abramov's reputation as the first of the new group of 'country writers'.

Five years after *Brothers and Sisters*, however, Abramov fell into disfavour for a while. This was after the publication in the Leningrad magazine *Neva* of his story *Around and About*.[4] The hero of this story, set in 1962, is a hard-pressed *kolkhoz* chairman. His bosses on the regional Party committee send him orders which are quite impossible to carry out, partly because of the lack of manpower in his village, but even more because of the total lack of enthusiasm on the part of his farmworkers. It is August, and the *kolkhoz* has not made any labour-day payments yet this year, either in cash or in kind. So the farmworkers are shamming sick, staying at home to grow vegetables on their allotments and then selling their produce in the open market to get a little cash. When the chairman tries to get them out into the fields on a Sunday to save the hay crop threatened by rain, they say why should we bother, when you won't give us enough hay to keep our own cows? One of the brigade-leaders has taken to drink, out of bitter resentment that the State is not treating him as a full citizen. Why has he no passport, while factory workers have them? he asks. He is not being treated as a responsible human being; so he is not going to work like one. The unfortunate chairman, at his wits' end, reflects:

> In the district Party committee they say I'm a bad organiser, and I don't do enough educational propaganda work. But how can you get across propaganda to the *kolkhoz* worker nowadays? You can't do a thing with him unless you give him a few roubles. You can tell him: look, we had to buy two tractors this year, now we

> need lorries and new cowsheds, then we'll put in piped radio – and after that we'll get around to the labour-day payments. But the *kolkhoznik* won't wait. He's no longer willing to wait – and that's my problem now.

The story ends with the chairman drowning his woes at the village café, where he gets extremely drunk and promises the workers that if they save the hay for him, they can have thirty per cent of the crop for themselves (the official rule is that they are allowed to keep only ten per cent). As a result, when next day he staggers out to the hayfield with a hangover, he finds everyone hard at work. But what is he going to tell his Party bosses? He is the thirteenth chairman of this *kolkhoz* since the war, and it looks as though there will soon be a fourteenth.

Not surprisingly, this gloomy account of life down on the farm in the early 1960s caused considerable offence in Party circles. Abramov's hero had after all even raised the question of whether forcible collectivisation in the 1930s had perhaps been a mistake. An officially-inspired press campaign started up, in the course of which *Izvestiya* printed a letter from the inhabitants of Abramov's home village, protesting against his portrayal of their life. But Abramov did not become a dissident writer: he weathered the storm of criticism and a few years later, in 1968, *Novy Mir* printed the second part of his saga about the Pryaslin family in the northern village of Pekashino.[5] Once again the reactions of Abramov's characters to the hardships of their life are not stereotyped – they ring true. But he was wise enough to make it quite clear that he was writing about a Soviet village twenty years earlier – so that any unpleasant phenomena he described could be presumed to be the result of Stalin's policies. Thus we find the hero of the novel, Mikhail Pryaslin, expressing his resentment at being trapped in the village, unable to get out into the wide world. But the date is the summer of 1947, and Mikhail, aged twenty, is giving advice to his young twin brothers, aged eleven:

> 'What are you going to be when you grow up?' Mikhail asked.
> Petka glanced shyly at Grishka. 'We'll be like you . . .'
> 'What do you mean, like me?'
> 'Later on – we'll be like you are now . . .'

Mikhail shook his head. 'No, no, kids. Look at me – I'm twenty, and what have I seen, where have I been? Life is great, and our country is huge. You need to study – I didn't get the chance, and neither did your sister . . .'

'How could I study?' Liza broke in. 'I'd be sitting learning a school lesson, and all the time I'd be worrying about the cow and whether there was enough grass for her, or wondering where the little ones had got to.'

'That's you she was worrying about,' said Mikhail. 'So you see, you've got to study to make up for me and for her . . . You're growing up in different times: everything's better now, *you* won't have to leave school at fourteen and go off timber-felling . . . I always dreamed of transferring from a horse and cart to a tractor, I wanted to go on a tractor-drivers' course – but it didn't come off.'

'The war spoilt Mikhail's life,' Liza told the twins. 'The war, and us younger ones. They wouldn't take him for the army because of us – we would have died of hunger without him. So remember that, never forget it, wherever you go and whatever you become later on.'

The better days that lie ahead for the Pryaslin twins are, however, still a distant dream in 1947. The reality of life in this remote northern village, two years after the end of the war, is grim and hungry. The few men in the village are mostly war cripples; the *kolkhoz* pays its workers very little; children are dying of tuberculosis because there is no milk for them. And in this situation a State Loan is launched throughout the country. A local Party official named Ganichev arrives in Pekashino to pressurise the *kolkhoz* workers into subscribing to the loan. Abramov describes Ganichev's unsuccessful attempt to squeeze a cash contribution out of one *kolkhoz* worker, Pyotr Zhitov. Pyotr came home from the war with a wooden leg, and when Ganichev calls at his house he finds him on a drinking spree – he had started during the May Day holiday, and then continued in honour of the funeral of a neighbour. The drink has loosened Zhitov's tongue, and he pushes his wooden leg forward aggressively to make sure that Ganichev notices it.

'Wife, how many labour-days did I clock up last year?'

'350.'

'And this year?'

'Ninety so far.'

'That's since January, not counting April when I was sent off timber-felling. Not a bad record, eh, comrade? Don't you think Pyotr Zhitov is worthy of the title – Invalid of the Great Patriotic War? Does everyone else work as hard as me in this *kolkhoz*?'

Ganichev said, 'Yes, you're a good worker, one could call you a Stakhanovite, even.'

'And Pyotr Zhitov will be a Stakhanovite in subscribing to the loan, too! What's the biggest subscription you've had so far, Comrade Ganichev? How much did First Secretary Podrezov sign for?'

'Why do you want to know?'

'Because I want to make an effort equal to the greatest. Did he sign for two months' salary?'

After a pause, Ganichev nodded. 'Right, two months' worth from the First Secretary. Well, so I'll sign for three months' salary – does that suit you? And I'll pay it all now, in cash. Wife, where is our cash?'

And without waiting for his wife, who was sitting behind a screen, having just finished breast-feeding a child, Zhitov got up and took down an old school copybook from a shelf over the table. With a blue carpenter's pencil he started to make some calculations. When he finished, he said: 'Write it down, Comrade Ganichev: 90 labour-days and 13 roubles 50 kopecks.'

Ganichev forced himself to smile. 'You wouldn't have made a bad actor, Zhitov.'

'You think so?'

'Yes. But we haven't come here to watch a comedy.'

'Really, Comrade Ganichev!' Pyotr Zhitov protested. 'Here I am, signing on for three months' pay, and you talk like that. Look here' – he took up his pencil again – 'last year I chalked up 350 labour-days, and this year I think I'll be working just as many. Make it a round figure – I don't want to be mean – say 360. Divide 360 days by twelve and you get thirty; so for three months the figure will be ninety – is that right? Right, now for the money. This year they haven't paid anything per labour-day so far – all right, let's reckon it up by last year, when they gave sometimes eleven, sometimes fifteen kopecks per labour-day. Multiply fifteen by ninety, and we get 13 roubles 50 kopecks by my reckoning. You can check it yourself, Comrade Ganichev.'

'Don't play the fool, Zhitov – stop trying to be clever. This can't be the first time you've subscribed to a loan, and you know we never accept labour-days in payment.'

'O-ho – so you don't accept *kolkhoz* currency? Just tell me then, Comrade Ganichev, what is this *kolkhoz* currency worth?' And Pyotr Zhitov banged his fist on the table.

To put an end to this pointless discussion with a drunken man, the *kolkhoz* chairman Lukashin pointed out that Pyotr Zhitov did also have, besides his labour-days, some cash income – he had, after all, worked in the forest during April. And Ganichev added: 'You also get a disabled person's pension.'

'Quite right, so I do – 112 roubles a month. And do you know how much my old parents get? And who has to feed them? Let's discuss that too.'

'First of all I think we should discuss your tongue, and how to put a curb on it.'

'All right, all right: you try to get everything by frightening people, Comrade Ganichev. But I've been frightened already, as you ought to know' – and Pyotr Zhitov lifted his wooden leg and tapped it with his fist below the knee. 'Can you hear my music?'

So Ganichev has to leave Pyotr Zhitov's house without reaching any agreement about his subscription to the State Loan.

Meanwhile Abramov's main hero, Mikhail Pryaslin, is more and more unhappy and frustrated. The Pryaslin family cow dies, the younger children need milk, and to get the money to buy another cow Mikhail has to agree to his sister Liza marrying a man he knows is no good (and who in fact soon deserts her). Abramov describes Mikhail's frame of mind on the evening after Liza's wedding:

Pekashino was sleeping now, tired after the long day – not a single light in any of the houses. Only Mikhail wandered like a lost soul round the village by night. Why couldn't he sleep, he asked himself? The ball was over, as a book he'd once read put it: it was done now, no amount of tearing his hair could change anything. Suddenly a cheering thought came to him: what if it was love? Why was he tormenting himself, thinking Liza had sacrificed herself to save the family? Maybe it really was love, and she was happy that she had married Egor? . . . Far away at the foot of the hill, just at the bend in the river, a red light shone brightly. Was it someone fishing illegally at night? Or someone secretly setting off to seek his fortune in strange lands? A lot of people nowadays were running off to the towns. And what was he, Mikhail, going to do? How he hated this time of year: every time autumn came round the question arose, as inevitable as the snow and the frost – how was he to go on living, where could he go? Fish hibernate for the winter down in the depths of the river; squirrels go off to find their stores of nuts in the fir-groves; birds fly away to warmer lands. And what of him? Why couldn't he spread his wings and fly away? After all, he was twenty years old. As though to excite and inspire him, a bright shooting star traced its path through the night sky above his head. Then the star burst, and in its greenish light he saw his own house, low to the ground, painfully familiar, its roof coated in frost.

That extract was from Abramov's novel *Two Winters and Three Summers*, which appeared in *Novy Mir* in 1968. The next instalment, *Roads and Crossroads*, came out five years later and dealt with events in the village of Pekashino in 1951.[6] Now the villagers' grumblings are louder than ever, and even the Party officials are beginning to join in. Early in the book the local First Party Secretary Podrezov comes to dinner with the *kolkhoz* chairman, Lukashin. Lukashin's wife Anfisa drinks a vodka toast, and then bursts into a spirited attack on the Party's failure to fulfil its promises:

'I haven't forgotten how you came here in 1942. Do you remember what you told us then? Just hang on a little longer, women (you said) – after the war you'll have plenty to eat. But it's six years since the war ended, and we women are still hanging on, still can't eat our fill . . . Ration books were abolished years ago, and yet there's still no bread in the shops. How long is this going to go on?'

Kolkhoz chairman and Party Secretary, who are old friends, go off on a fishing trip together, and, sitting by the camp-fire with no one to overhear them, talk freely about the situation on the farms. Party Secretary Podrezov admits:

'We had four years of war, and six years have passed since then – that makes ten years that people have had one thing only on their minds: where the next piece of bread was coming from.'

'And if we go on like this, they'll go on going short for another ten years,' Lukashin said. 'Look what's happening: the State takes all my milk and gives me eleven kopecks for what cost me two roubles to produce. Yet it was Lenin who said, after the civil war, that proper relations should be established with the villages, that not everything should be taken from the peasant. As a *kolkhoz* boss I can't do anything but crack the whip: I've nothing to give people. But a horse needs oats to make it go. What good is a hungry man as a worker? You know, we used to have a *kulak* in our village years ago, Ivan Kropotov – now, *he* understood the basic law of economics. You know what he used to say to his wife every morning – and she was a miserly old bag – "Feed the workers till they're full," he'd say: that was his first order every morning. He knew that a man who's eaten his fill can move mountains, but a hungry man is just a drag.'

Roads and Crossroads ends in the autumn of 1952. The *kolkhoz* chairman Lukashin is arrested: desperate for some material incentives to get his workers to finish building new cowsheds before the winter, he gave them an unauthorised grain issue. But the *kolkhoz*'s grain deliveries to the State had not been completed and someone reported him for anti-State activities. Mikhail Pryaslin goes round the village to get signatures to a collective letter in support of Lukashin. Most people refuse to sign, afraid it will get them into trouble. But finally one of the few Party members in the village, Ilya Netyosov, signs the letter, and Mikhail feels this is the turning-point and things will now improve. The novel ends like this:

> In the sky the cranes were flying, their melancholy cries sounding like an apology – 'we're off to warmer lands, while you have to stay and stick it out here'. It was a grey day – the cranes always seemed to leave on a day like this. But Mikhail did not feel his usual sadness at their departure. He stood on the steps of Netyosov's house, his strong legs planted wide apart like a true peasant. He gazed at the wedge-shaped skein of cranes disappearing into the distance, and before his eyes there rose a vision of his native land – stretching widely, covered with the green powdering of the young winter crops. It was he, all these hard years, he and the women of Pekashino, who had raised their country up from its ruins, had rebuilt and fed the towns. And now a new, proud feeling of being the *master* was growing ever stronger within him.

Abramov wrote that in 1973, and it does not ring very true: it is hard to believe that any Soviet peasant actually felt like that in 1952, the year before Stalin's death. But this theme – the peasant claiming the right to run his own life – has been cropping up constantly over the years since then, both in fiction and in straight press reports about the countryside. In the last volume of the Pryaslin saga, called *The House* and published at the end of 1978,[7] Abramov's hero has a family of his own and a new house with electricity and piped radio. But the *kolkhoz* is still suffering from impossible instructions issued by inept local Party bosses. Mikhail and his fellow-workers no longer suffer these in silence, but they are still not able to make full use of the right which Abramov points out is theirs as working members of a collective – to be their own boss.

Another writer with a deep sympathy for the Russian peasantry was Efim Dorosh. Older than Abramov, he wrote in great detail of rural life in the 1950s and 1960s. He died in 1972. His *Country Diary*, the first instalment of which came out in *Novy Mir* in 1964, is a documentary chronicle of life in a small provincial town and its surrounding *kolkhozy*, in the years from 1954 up to 1970. Running all through this chronicle is Dorosh's passionate belief in the Russian peasant's shrewdness and capacity for hard work – qualities which he feels are often frustrated by those in authority, instead of being harnessed to raise the general level of agriculture.

His imaginary provincial town, Raigorod, is 100 kilometres from Moscow, in the centre of an area which by tradition grows vegetables and fruit. But thanks to the inefficiency of the collective farms the local people are forced into earning money on the side. In 1954, for instance, Dorosh notes that on one *kolkhoz* all the women workers took a week off in July to sell their cherries in the town's open market. If they were paid a proper cash rate for their labour-days, he comments, they would not need to do this – instead they could get the collective hay harvest finished. A lot of the inhabitants of Raigorod, he writes disapprovingly, are former farmworkers who have taken jobs as night-watchmen in order to have time to grow cucumbers and tomatoes on their allotments. Moreover, when they take their produce to Moscow to sell, they fill up the suburban trains and then form queues in the Moscow shops to buy goods such as white bread or sugar which are not available back in Raigorod. Dorosh cites the case of one young man who got himself registered as a member of a fishing co-operative on the nearby lake, but who had made so much money from selling fish privately that he was buying a Moskvich car in order to extend his profit-making operations further afield. And *he* was educated as a good Komsomol member, Dorosh comments in horror.

That was all in 1954. In another instalment which relates to 1959,[8] Dorosh reports that the distribution system is working better, but regrets that religious prejudices still linger on in the countryside. In one passage the author goes with his friend Ivan Fedoseyevich (chairman of a local *kolkhoz*) into a general store in the large village of Ugozhi:

> It was semi-dark in the shop, and smelt of all kinds of groceries. The low ceiling and thick brick walls exuded a welcome coolness on this hot summer day. Two salesgirls were busy at the counters. One was selling salt herring, butter, salt, sausage; the other – wine, sugar, sweets, gingerbread. They also had on sale big fresh strawberries, at only half the price they were charging in Raigorod. Ivan Fedoseyevich asked where they came from, and the girl said – from our *sovkhoz*. She apologised for some of the berries being a little muddied – there had been heavy rain the previous night. She asked what we would like and

> offered us various goods – some tins of Bulgarian stuffed cabbage, for instance, had just come in, she said. Ivan Fedoseyevich told how during the Lenten fast he had fed his mother on those tins, telling her they contained only cabbage and kasha. The old lady ate it with pleasure, remarking on how well she had got through Lent this time, not feeling at all weak after all those weeks without meat. Then Ivan Fedoseyevich confessed to her that there *had* been some meat in the stuffing. But his mother was not at all upset, and merely said, 'Oh well, the sin is yours, not mine . . .'

Dorosh makes it very clear that his *kolkhoz* chairman friend was not himself a believer. But he knew when the various religious feasts were due, and was well aware that those were the times you could find people at home, since they all took a holiday then. For instance, every summer there was the two-day Tikhvin holiday:

> Naturally the miraculous appearance of the icon of the Tikhvin Mother of God, which was first revealed to believers in Constantinople, and which in the days of Dmitri Donskoi was supposed to have come floating across the waters of Lake Ladoga to the Tikhvin River, where a monastery was later built – all this meant absolutely nothing to Ivan Fedoseyevich. But still he was enough of a peasant to feel it was not right to go visiting people on working days, and to remember the village feast-days even though their meaning was now non-existent for him.

Efim Dorosh's picture of Russian provincial life was somewhat idealised, but his diagnosis of inefficiencies in the system of agriculture remains largely accurate in the 1980s. He wrote, for instance, that it ought to be perfectly possible to get asparagus grown in Raigorod on to dinner-tables in Moscow five hours later – but this dream seems to have vanished without trace, defeated by the Soviet distribution system. Twenty years later, *kolkhoz* workers are still making money from their private plots just as Dorosh described, and Soviet towns are still so short of fresh meat, fruit and vegetables that official encouragement is now being given to the private sector. In the summer of 1982 a barelyfictionalised story by Mikhail Kolosov[9] told how the attitude of the authorities has changed over the years on this subject. The hero Ivan spent his working life as a railway-maintenance mechanic, living in a railway settlement where he was allowed to keep a cow and pigs, and supplying his relatives in town with the produce. In 1957, however, it was forbidden to keep animals in towns or workers' settlements; so Ivan sold his cow to the local *kolkhoz* and killed his piglets. Not until he was getting arthritic, and both his children had married and left home, were private livestock allowed again. Then the same official who in 1957 came round measuring the private plots and reducing them in size came back and urged Ivan to keep a cow again, since the country needed more meat. It's too late, Ivan said at first; the children have left, and anyway they don't like dirt or hard physical work, they would rather buy their milk from a shop. But in the end his son needs money to buy a co-operative flat in town, and to get it he comes home to dig Ivan's plot and plant onions to sell in the market. So Ivan buys two piglets and starts again.

Soviet sociologists have written many articles recently on the changing psychology of country dwellers: for instance, their unwillingness to spend long hours looking after a family cow, and their raised expectations of comfort in their daily life – which means fixed hours with a minimum of overtime, mains water and electricity, and above all an individual house or cottage for each family, often built and owned by the occupiers. This craving to own a house of one's own is also felt by town-dwellers who would like to acquire a second home for holiday use. A comparatively new phenomenon, this often leads to conflicts with local authorities – as is reflected in some of the recently published stories. The Omsk writer Anatoli Chernousov, for instance, wrote a story, *The Second Home*,[10] in which the hero Andrei Gorchakov spends a whole summer building a holiday house in a remote village in the Urals. He and his friends want to spend their summers in the village, growing vegetables which they would take back to town with them in the autumn. The State can only benefit from this – as another summer-house owner (*dachnik*) puts it:

> I can foresee that in the future a lot of townsmen are going to become half townsmen, half peasants . . . Many of them will

> either work a plot of land, or raise some kind of livestock – hens, pigs, rabbits. Everything is pointing that way . . . The *kolkhozy* and *sovkhozy* will remain the basic agricultural producers, and the half-townsmen, half-peasants will merely help them out. There are a lot of small pieces of land, little fields, which at present are uneconomic . . . They could be handed over to townsmen who want them – let them dig the earth to the benefit of themselves, their children and society.

The *dachniki* in Chernousov's story move into the village and build themselves houses of many different types, satisfying their urge for something different, something of one's own, an urge which cannot find expression in standardised town flats. But they have to get their building materials illegally, and some of them are rogues: for instance, the director of a big-town food store, who puts up a stone house behind a high fence, equips it with swimming pool and colour TV, and pays his workmen in short-supply sausages. Finally disaster looms ahead for all the new inhabitants of this village: the chairman of the local council (*sel'soviet*) arrives one day and announces that a rest centre for a local town enterprise is to be built on the site of the village. The original local residents will be moved to accommodation elsewhere, and all the *dachniki* must move out, since they are using state land illegally. If they don't move, their houses will be bulldozed. But it is only fair to add that Chernousov wrote that story in 1983. It is certain that no real-life local council would behave in such a way today, with the launch of Gorbachev's campaign encouraging urban dwellers to acquire allotments and grow vegetables on them.

Most Soviet townsmen are the sons or grandsons of peasants, so that their ties with the countryside have not been completely severed, and although career prospects, educational facilities, and comforts such as shops or mod. cons. all tend to keep people in the cities, there has been a noticeable growth in what could be called the Russian 'Back to the Land' movement over the last twenty years. Sympathisers with this movement are torn between nostalgia for the old village customs and neighbourly way of life, and repulsion against the traditional disadvantages of Russian country life such as lack of roads, ignorance and drunkenness. One of the best-known stories of country life revealing this duality, was *Vologda*

Wedding[11] by the poet Alexander Yashin published over twenty years ago in *Novy Mir*. It is a semi-documentary account of a village wedding in northern Russia. Readers of *Novy Mir* who were critical of the regime loved this story for its bitter truths about life out in the sticks, while a much broader circle of readers loved Yashin's use of genuine peasant idiom in his dialogue, and his description of old wedding customs still being observed in a Soviet village. Yashin himself came from the Vologda area; he once described his home village as 'lost in the remote forests' – it had no electricity and the roads were impassable in spring and autumn. His mother and sister were still living there, and still illiterate, when Yashin died in 1968. This story is about his cousin's wedding in that village in the winter of 1961–2, and it starts with the author's long journey home from Moscow. It takes him twelve hours by train, then forty-five minutes by plane over the forest, then the last few kilometres on skis. When he gets there he finds a two-day wedding feast in full swing. It's a big village, but there are no radio sets, no library, no club or cinema, so a wedding is a major form of entertainment for everyone, even in a 30-degree frost. The bridegroom and his friends come to fetch the bride in a lorry: at the entrance to the village they are stopped at a wooden barrier, and have to pay the bride's ransom – in sweets, wine and money. Back at the bride's home, her girl-friends are singing merrily in the kitchen while urging the bride to weep loudly – she is supposed to lament at being taken from her mother. Yashin gets himself a drink and settles down to observe what goes on:

> At any feasting, the most important thing is the people. People's characters are revealed as the festivities get under way, and at any village celebration there are always people dancing or weeping, arguing or talking nonsense. Some are silent, others shouting, the young women are singing, the widows are shedding tears. And amongst the men present on any such occasion there are sure to be several of those typically Russian seekers-after-truth, who are always going on about the need for justice and happiness for all. These people have plenty of critical observations to make – about the Germans, the Americans, the Turks, and most of all about their own fellow-countrymen. Men like this have no time for merriment, for singing or

dancing; they are too busy denouncing, accusing, demanding retribution, protesting – and asking all the time: what should we do? What happens next? Whose fault is it? And do those great men who stand above us *know* about our troubles, are they aware of *everything*? No doubt their persistence in this sort of talk is a reflection of the Russian national character; but heaven help you if you ever have to spend a whole evening in the power of one of these firebrands, for he won't let you take any part in the feasting, you'll see nothing and hear nothing of it . . .

Among the colourful characters at this particular wedding is an old *kolkhoz* worker who goes round the table taking out his plastic dentures and showing them to everyone – 'Just look how I can chew with them, I can crunch bones even – and they were made here, in this district!' Other wedding guests are talking about their animals: 'A goat's far better than a cow, it'll eat anything, even propaganda posters and newspapers!' As they all get drunk, some people get nicer and some nastier. Some of the women are weeping, remembering dead sons and husbands – but there are some merry widows too, who were delighted to be rid of their despotic husbands and who are now free to run their own lives. The bridegroom's uncle, who has had two prison sentences for hooliganism, gets very drunk and has to be tied up on the first evening and given a sedative in his beer on the second evening. The bride's brother goes round filling up the glasses. Besides himself and his sister, his mother had seven other children, but they all died as babies because she worked so hard; they were all born out in the fields while she was at work – this would have been in the 1920s and 1930s. The bridegroom gets roaring drunk and shouts, 'I'm Chapai, I'm Chapai! – are you listening, Galya?' and the bride replies, 'All right, all right, you're Chapai – but just remember I earn more than you do' (they both work at the local flax mill). When all the beer in the bride's home has been drunk, the wedding feast transfers by lorry to the bridegroom's home, forty kilometres away in another village. The feast ends on the third morning, when the bride ceremonially sweeps the floor in her new home, and serves pancakes to her relatives and guests.

Yashin's *Vologda Wedding* was published in *Novy Mir* in 1962, and it was followed in the pages of the same journal by several more, equally truthful stories of country life. This was during Tvardovsky's second period as editor, when he was able to publish in *Novy Mir* not only Solzhenitsyn's *One Day in the Life of Ivan Denisovich* but also his *Matryona's Home* with its portrayal of an old illiterate peasant woman, despised by her materialist-minded relatives, who was for Solzhenitsyn 'that righteous one without whom no village can stand – nor any city – nor our whole land'. Tvardovsky also printed stories of village life by Vasili Shukshin, who was born in a peasant family in the Altai region, and made a brilliant if short career as writer, film producer and actor: he died in 1974. One of Shukshin's first stories, *Stepka*, came out in *Novy Mir* in 1964.[12] The hero is a simple peasant lad who serves five years in a labour camp (he was sentenced after a drunken brawl), and then comes home to his native village earlier than expected. His dumb sister and his elderly parents are overjoyed to see him; friends come in to celebrate his return, bringing food and drink since the family is a poor one. Stepka boasts about how good life was in the camp: they used to have political lectures, film shows twice a week, enough food to eat, interesting people to talk to, no thieving from one another, even women among the prisoners. All this is contrasted by implication with life in his home village. But the celebrations are interrupted by the arrival of the local militiaman, who has come to arrest Stepka. It turns out that three months before he was due for release he escaped, together with two long-term criminals, simply out of homesickness. The militiaman can't understand him. 'You only had three months to go,' he says, 'and now they'll give you another two years.' Stepka answers: 'Never mind – I'm all right now, I can stand another two years. Before, I used to dream of the village every night. It's nice here in the spring, isn't it?' And he goes off back to the camp, leaving his poor dumb sister weeping.

Another Shukshin story, this time from 1967, is called *In Profile and Full-Face*.[13] A village lad named Ivan comes home after service in the navy, and is employed as a *kolkhoz* driver. But one day he is found driving while drunk, his licence is removed for a year, and the *kolkhoz* chairman puts him to work mucking out the cowsheds. Unable to stand the prospect of the next few months, Ivan decides to run away to join a friend who is working as a miner in the south. Before he goes he talks to an old villager, who gives him a lecture on how young people nowadays don't know what real work is. Ivan's comment: 'It was all right for you, you were only half-conscious in those days. But I can't live like that: I want something more out of life. Not money, I don't want just to work to fill my stomach, I want something to live for.' You should get married, says the old man – then you wouldn't have time to think up nonsense. But Ivan won't listen; he goes away, leaving his widowed mother on her own.

Shukshin and Solzhenitsyn both wrote with particular sympathy of the lot of the older village women, bowed down with the burden of household chores and usually abandoned by their children and left to face a lonely old age. Another writer who is fascinated by both the speech and the philosophy of old country ladies is Valentin Rasputin, the best of the 'country writers' school, whose stories about characters from his native Siberia are beginning to be known in the West in translation. In his story *Farewell to Matyora*,[14] an old woman named Dariya goes to the village graveyard and asks the dead lying there – why am I alive?

> Who knows the truth about man, the reason why he is alive? Does a man live just for himself, for his children and his children's children, or for something more? And what ought a man to feel about the earlier generations, who lived that he might live? What can we tell our children when they ask us why we gave them birth?

Dariya is driven to ask such questions because she is about to lose her home on an island in the Siberian Angara river. The river is being dammed further down to give power for a new hydroelectric station, and the island of Matyora will be drowned – and with it the graves of Dariya's ancestors. She argues with her grandson Andrei, who tells her, 'It's progress, grandma, we must all move with the times.' 'That's the trouble with you young people,' she replies, 'you're all far too busy moving, and you're so busy filling your bellies that you forget you have souls.'

Dariya suggests that Andrei and his clever friends should invent a machine that could cut the island of Matyora from its foundations, tow it to the edge of the lake that is about to be formed, and moor it next to the dry land. The suggestion makes the young people smile, but the philosophy behind it is serious:

> The earth doesn't belong to you young people alone, it belongs to everyone – to those who came before us and to those who will come after us. We all live on this earth only a short time. We were given Matyora to maintain, to look after and to feed ourselves from. But now look what you're doing with it! Your elders handed it down to you – but you are wasting God's gift. And it's not us, your elders, that you must answer to: it's your children.

Farewell to Matyora is a long story, marvellously written, moving slowly on through the island's last days, in the summer and autumn before the waters cover it. At the end of the story a group of old people are left on the island, marooned in a thick fog, waiting for the waters to rise while the boat that has come to take them off is unable to find them. Rasputin likes to leave his stories open-ended and his readers still thinking about the questions he raises. This is true, for instance, of his story *Money for Maria*,[15] which combines a gloomy picture of contemporary village life and some equally gloomy reflections on how the villagers' characters have changed for the worse. It is about Maria, a simple, uneducated woman who runs the village store, gets the accounts in a muddle and is faced with a shortfall of a thousand roubles. She will get a prison sentence unless her husband Kuz'ma can find the money within five days. So Kuz'ma goes round the village begging, with not much success: his appeals to help Maria are a touchstone to people's characters – those who have money are mean with it, while others make a big gesture in front of their colleagues and give Kuz'ma a large sum – and then come privately to beg the money back again. One old pensioner, Gordei (who has no money, but borrows fifteen roubles from his son for Kuz'ma), delivers a stinging attack on people who think too much about money:

> When did it happen in the old days that village people took money for helping one another? If someone was building a house or putting in a new stove, people would come to help him; if the host had some hooch he brought it out, if not – 'never mind, next time I'll come and help *you*'. But nowadays it's all done for money: ten roubles to dig your allotment, ten roubles to bring in your hay – they work for money, and by money they live. They're looking for a profit all the time.

The husband, Kuz'ma, has an old-fashioned attitude to money: if it's there, spend it, if not – do without. He earns little cash, and until now has needed very little. Maria's pay clothes the four children, they get a corn issue from the *kolkhoz*, and they have their own milk and meat. Most of his neighbours, he knows, are in the same situation; but some of them have been saving up to buy motor-cycles, and he starts out full of confidence that they will loan him their savings. After three days he realises that his hopes were unfounded. So he takes a long train journey to visit his brother, whom he has not seen for seven years but who has made good in the town and is now well off. On the way he meets a variety of people, some of whom worship money and some not. Rasputin leaves the ending in the balance, but one feels he is very fond of this hero who clings desperately to his faith in the goodness of human nature. Kuz'ma arrives in the strange town, still hopeful, goes by bus and on foot through the snow to his brother's flat, and rings the bell. His words end the story: 'Here I am – say a prayer now, Maria! In a moment, the door will open.'

Money for Maria was one of Rasputin's early stories, published in 1968. In his much more recent story, *The Fire*,[16] he returns to the theme of the decline of moral standards among country people whose lives have been disrupted by modern technology. His hero, Ivan Egorov, comes from another Siberian village like Matyora, drowned when the Angara river was dammed.

Some time in the 1960s, Egorov and his fellow-villagers migrated to Sosnovka, a timber-felling settlement where at first they stayed in their old communities, each living in their own street and each preserving the old tradition of village unity, looking after the weaker members of the group. But twenty years have passed: many of the original settlers in Sosnovka have died or moved on, and they have been replaced by people from the towns who are only interested in making money. Ivan reflects that in his youth in the village, good and evil used to be clearly defined, but now they are all mixed up. It used to be considered that a good man was someone who felt for another's misery; but nowadays a good man is someone who doesn't interfere with others, who does no evil but also does no good. When a fire breaks out in the settlement and destroys all the warehouses, Ivan is one of the few who carry the food and goods to safety without helping himself:

everyone else is busily looting the vodka, wine, butter and sugar, and an old watchman is killed when he tries to prevent them doing so. Next day, as everyone awaits the arrival of the police to investigate the death, and the commission whose members will count up how many boxes of vodka are missing, Ivan leaves Sosnovka to find work elsewhere. He walks off into the forest, 'a small man who has lost his way and despairs of ever finding his home . . .'

Rasputin's deeply pessimistic story might lead a reader to conclude that the outlook for Russian village life is unrelievedly gloomy. This is obviously not the opinion of Russians who have decided to reverse the trend so noticeable in the 1930s and in the first post-war years, when everyone who could do so escaped from the villages to find work in towns. Nowadays, it seems, there are quite a few townsmen moving back to the country – not just as weekenders, but to work and live there permanently. An example of one who made the switch successfully is the hero of a story by Ivan Vinogradov with the charming title *A solo on the shepherd's pipes*.[17]

Pyotr Kuzmich is a military engineer who is invalided out of the service in his forties with a serious heart attack. He decides to abandon the stressful city life of Leningrad and go back to his roots in a village in the province of Pskov. His native hamlet has been closed down and is now buried under weeds, and his parents are dead. But the director of the local *sovhoz* is an old friend who gives Pyotr a summer job as shepherd, looking after the herd of privately-owned cows and sheep belonging to the farmworkers. At first Pyotr sets out in the morning at the head of the flock to music from a transistor radio, but the batteries soon give out, and then he cuts reeds and makes a shepherd's pipe or *zhaleika* to play to the cows. It is a peaceful summer, interrupted only when a cow falls into a deep bog, or a mad wolf kills one of the sheep. In the autumn Pyotr and his wife return to their noisy Leningrad flat: but he finds he cannot stand urban life any more, and the following summer he moves out for good. In the army his job had been planning and supervising the construction of military camps, bridges and so on: now he gets the job of organising the building of individual cottages for farm employees. The story ends with Pyotr happily dreaming of building his own log-house on a hillock covered with heather: it will have big windows, a high slate roof, a verandah, and an upper room with wide views over meadows and stream, where perhaps he will sit and paint water-colours or write his memoirs, in his old age.

All sorts of technical difficulties have to be overcome by Russians who would like to buy or build a house in the country. You are not supposed to own a house in a village unless you are registered as living there, so first you must get a job locally, and then apply for a plot of land. Building materials are in short supply, particularly wood: recent legislation includes a ban on indiscriminate tree-felling. The solution often is to buy a ruined shack in an abandoned village, and transport it to the site of your new intended abode. This was the way chosen by Viktor, a factory mechanic in a small town in the Vladimir province and hero of the story *Grandfather's House* by Sergei Golitsyn.[18] Viktor inherits his grandfather's wooden house, which now stands in an outlying district of the town, where all the buildings are due to be bulldozed and the area re-developed. The house had started life in a village, and had been brought to town with the grandfather forty years ago, when he came to work in the factory. Now his grandson Viktor wants to reverse the process and move the house back to the country. His grandfather's old village has vanished, so Viktor finds a fictitious granny, an old woman in the town who used to live in a village, and who makes an official request for permission to move back there. The old lady stays on in her town flat, while Viktor speedily replaces her decayed hut with his grandfather's house, cultivates the plot of land around the hut, and starts growing hothouse cucumbers. His original intention was to use the house as a second home, but he is so persecuted by the local council bureaucrats for breaking minor regulations that in the end he leaves his town job, gets work as a mechanic with the local *sovhoz*, and is finally accepted as a new villager.

Golitsyn's story ends with the statement that many other town-dwellers are preparing to follow Viktor's example and move out of town. Viktor has many thousands of real-life prototypes, and the advent of these individualistic, energetic devotees of the Good Life must surely help to reinvigorate the villages and counteract the trends towards rural decay so depressingly chronicled by Abramov or Rasputin.

REFERENCES

1 Vasili Belov, *Mazurik* (*Novy Mir* 1968, no. 2).
2 Dmitri Mikhleyev, *Krugovorot* (*Yunost* 1983, no. 2).
3 Fyodor Abramov, *Brat'ya i sestry* (*Novy Mir* 1958).
4 Fyodor Abramov, *Vokrug da okolo* (*Neva* 1963).
5 Fyodor Abramov, *Dve zimy i tri leta* (*Novy Mir* 1968, nos. 1–3).
6 Fyodor Abramov, *Puti i pereput'ya* (*Novy Mir* 1973, nos. 1–3).
7 Fyodor Abramov, *Dom* (*Novy Mir* 1978, no. 12).
8 Efim Dorosh, *Derevenski dnevnik* (*Novy Mir* 1964, no. 6).
9 Mikhail Kolosov, *I sebe i lyudyam* (*Oktyabr* 1982, no. 7).
10 Anatoli Chernousov, *Vtoroi dom* (*Nash Sovremennik* 1983, no. 1).
11 Alexander Yashin, *Vologodskaya svad'ba* (*Novy Mir* 1962, no. 12).
12 Vasili Shukshin, *Stepka* (*Novy Mir* 1964, no. 11).
13 Vasili Shukshin, *V profil' i anfas* (*Novy Mir* 1967, no. 9).
14 Valentin Rasputin, *Proshchanie s Matyoroi* (*Druzhba Narodov* 1977, no. 3).
15 Valentin Rasputin, *Den'gi dlya Marii* (Collected stories, Moscow 1978).
16 Valentin Rasputin, *Pozhar* (*Nash Sovremennik* 1985, no. 7).
17 Ivan Vinogradov, *Solo na zhaleike* (*Neva* 1984, no. 5).
18 Sergei Golitsyn, *Dedov dom* (*Novy Mir* 1985, no. 9).

5 The Pressures on Intellectuals

The relations between the Soviet intelligentsia and the State have a fascinating history, but one that is much too complex to be fitted into the framework of this limited study of modern Soviet fiction. I shall confine myself to the evidence to be found in stories and novels of the last twenty years regarding some of the pressures which bear heavily on intellectuals, particularly writers and artists, in Soviet society. These pressures include a burden of guilt (in the case of older writers who managed to keep on the right side of the authorities during the Stalinist years); the temptation to do oneself some good by joining in a campaign of denunciation against a colleague; the constant fight against censorship; and the more humdrum pressures of everyday life – the daily struggle to get one's fair share of foreign consumer goods or trips abroad, and the need to 'keep up with the Ivanovs' in all sorts of ways.

The unpleasant practice of public denunciation was itself roundly denounced in an interesting story with a radio setting, *The Boarded-Up Dachas* by Galina Shergova, which *Novy Mir* published in 1978.[1] The title refers to a village not far from Moscow where writers and artists have their summer *dachas*, now boarded up for the winter months. One of these artists is a successful painter, Kirill Proskurov. He has a regular programme on Moscow Radio called 'The Artist and Our Times'. The day before one of his recording sessions, he is rung up by an influential official in the Artists' Union named Soloduyev, who suggests that in his next talk he should criticise the recent work of a fellow-artist and friend. Proskurov knows that this friend, Yuri Sivak, has fallen into disfavour lately – after a meeting in the Artists' Union where he openly criticised the head of a power clique, Dymov. But Proskurov is quite unprepared for the pressure which is now put upon him by the Artists' Union official. Soloduyev makes it quite clear that it has been decided to mount a campaign against Yuri Sivak, and that unless Proskurov includes some severe criticism of him in his next radio talk, there will be unpleasant consequences for himself. Proskurov protests that Sivak is an old friend, who was at college with him, and that he likes his work, even though Sivak's style is one that he would never attempt himself. But Soloduyev merely replies that it would be a pity if the forthcoming personal exhibition of Proskurov's work which is about to take place had to be cancelled.

Proskurov, whom Galina Shergova portrays in this story as a pretty loathsome character, gives in to the pressure and includes some sharp criticism of Sivak's work in his next radio script. At his next recording session, however, the woman editor of his programme at Moscow Radio, Ekaterina Moskvina, greets him without any of her usual enthusiasm. Through the glass of the recording cubicle, Proskurov can see her commenting on the talk to the producer, but he cannot hear what is being said. He thinks of telling Moskvina that he only agreed to write the talk this way because, if it had been done by someone else, they might have been even sharper and more telling in their criticisms of Sivak – whereas he had tried to bury his criticisms in a framework of generalisations. But in the end he says nothing, and hurries home after the recording without even listening through the tape. Two days later Moskvina rings him at home and says she is sorry, but her bosses have taken his programme off the air. Many months later, Proskurov hears what actually happened on the day of his last recording. Moskvina was summoned by her chief editor, Trofimenko, who had been rung up by Soloduyev from the Artists' Union, complaining that Moskvina had refused to broadcast an important programme, and that she had not consulted her superiors before banning it. Moskvina explained the situation, reminding Trofimenko that at the last Moscow artists' exhibition, he had been loud in his praises of Sivak's paintings. Trofimenko takes immediate and surprising action:

> Trofimenko appreciated the nuances of the matter without any need for long explanations. He lifted the phone and dialled Soloduyev's number.

'I've discovered what has been going on. They were quite right to ban the programme. We are the *Radio*, Comrade Soloduyev: we can't suddenly turn round and crucify a man, just like that... Yes, of course – some people like his work, some people don't – why don't you start up a discussion in a specialised magazine? That can only be useful for the artist. But we are the *Radio*. Millions of people listen to us... What's this Sivak done anyway – committed ideological mistakes or compromised himself in some way? What d'you mean – that's not the point?'

Moskvina heard Soloduyev at the other end of the phone say, with great emphasis: 'There is an opinion current in the Artists' Union, to the effect that Sivak's work ought to be condemned in the most radical terms.'

'All right,' said Trofimenko, 'it's an excellent thing when an opinion exists. But I have an opinion too: that we ought not to broadcast this programme.'

And they don't. Moscow Radio withstands the pressure from the Union of Artists, Proskurov's series is taken off the air, and he retires to his *dacha* near Moscow, there to be gnawed by pangs of conscience. Some time later, he is visited at his *dacha* by Ekaterina Moskvina. She has come to collect from him the tape of his talk, which should have been destroyed but which was kept for him by a girl engineer who was in love with him. The story ends on a high note of moral indignation: Proskurov offers to walk Moskvina back to the station when she returns to Moscow, but she rejects the suggestion with horror: 'Oh no – I don't want to be seen walking in the street with you.'

Could such things happen in Soviet real life? Are there really any Moscow Radio editors who feel entirely confident that their bosses would back them on programme decisions that run counter to the wishes of highly-placed cultural bureaucrats? Galina Shergova's story certainly reads like a piece of wishful thinking, and it is interesting that she makes it very clear in the text that the action took place a long time ago: Proskurov's talk was recorded, she writes, in February 1964 – eight months before the end of Khrushchev's comparatively liberal reign.

Shergova's anti-hero, Proskurov, was left to carry for the rest of his life his burden of guilt for denouncing a friend. There are still many elderly Russians alive who have had to live with feelings of guilt since the mid-1930s, when wittingly or unwittingly they sent friends or acquaintances to prison camps – sometimes by writing a denunciation, much more often by simply failing to speak up in defence of someone. The ranks of these men are thinning every year, but the memory of what they did (or failed to do) has not died out, and often affects the next generation very strongly. This is shown in the book by writer Alexander Zinoviev, *The Radiant Future*,[2] which is set in Moscow in the 1960s. Zinoviev is now a Russian émigré, and his books are published only in the West.

One of the characters, an adolescent girl, commits suicide when she discovers that the father she idolises denounced his best friend and former comrade in 1945. The friend spent twelve years in the Gulag network, but forgave his denouncer, and when he returned to Moscow he became an honorary and much-loved uncle to the girl. In other words, in this work of fiction the older generation was able to put the crimes of Stalin's time behind them, while the younger generation was still unable to come to terms with the past.

An unusual passage in an officially published Soviet novel, where someone returns from the camps and tries to take up his life again, occurs in the last novel by Yuri Trifonov, *A time and a place*,[3] which was published after his death in 1981. In one episode, Trifonov describes a reunion in Moscow between two childhood friends. One of them, Misha Teterin, has just been rehabilitated after nearly twenty years in camp and exile. The other, Boris Kiyanov, kept quiet when Misha was arrested, and is now an established writer of safe but boring novels. But when they meet again, Kiyanov's sense of guilt over the easy life he has had compared with his friend lies between them. The two old men wander off to a restaurant, where with the aid of vodka they catch up on each other's news and are greeted by various mutual friends – some of whom won't speak to Kiyanov, unjustly blaming him for Misha's arrest. But it proves impossible to revive the old friendship, and soon afterwards Kiyanov is found dead from an overdose.

Another victim of the Stalinist purges, this time not an intellectual but an Old Bolshevik from the working class, was portrayed in Fyodor Abramov's last book, *The House*,[4] published in 1978, five years before the author's death. One of the characters in this novel is a militant Party member of simple origins, Kalina Dunaev. He had been arrested in the 1930s, but survived a long term of imprisonment and came home to live out his last twenty years in his native village as a hero of the Revolution. When he dies, he is given a grand funeral with a military brass band and a twenty-five-rifle salute.

Abramov devotes a lot of space in this novel to Kalina's wife Evdokia, giving her story the sub-title 'The life of Evdokia the Martyr'. She is an uneducated peasant woman, who spent the war years cleaning out latrines after her husband was arrested as an enemy of the people. Her only son, determined to expiate his father's alleged guilt, is killed at the front. Then after the war, Evdokia goes on a pilgrimage round the camps of the Gulag system, looking for her husband. She finds him dying of dysentery in a camp in Kolyma, nurses him back to life, and brings him home when he is rehabilitated after Stalin's death. This is a story straight out of contemporary Soviet mythology, which Abramov tells as if it were a folk-tale – but one that could perhaps have really happened. Ignored by the Soviet critics, this tale was one senior writer's contribution to telling the truth about the victims of the purges.

Feelings of guilt over the Stalinist past may be a heavy burden on a few older writers, but of course there is another tradition which runs throughout the history of the Russian intelligentsia – that of contracting out of public life, declining to take any part in politics or in decision-making. Quite a few contemporary Moscow or Leningrad writers have been following Oblomov's example in this respect for many years. During the Revolution and the civil war it was rather difficult to refuse to take any part in what was going on, and any real-life intellectual who, like the fictional Yuri Zhivago, tried to stand aside from the struggle received short shrift. But even during the 1930s, despite collectivisation and the purges, and certainly since 1945, it has been possible for some individuals to immerse themselves in academic work, to write only for themselves or a few friends, and to stand on the side-lines – at the cost, of course, of renouncing any form of career or worldly success. As one distinguished Russian émigré, the lawyer Valeri Chalidze, has put it in an article in the émigré journal *Kontinent*:[5]

> From the ethical viewpoint adopted by the Russian intelligentsia, for a man who is accepted in the homes of intellectuals to occupy any kind of post connected with taking state decisions is considered shameful. Moreover, it is considered to be shameful, from the same ethical viewpoint, to display any normal human desire for success or for making a career for oneself. I remember my intellectual friends in Russia, for whom the very word 'career' was a swear-word, something disgraceful.

There is a picture of one such a-political, indecisive intellectual in a story by Georgi Baklanov, *The youngest brother.*[6] The hero of the story is a history professor, Ilya Konstantinovich, now in his mid-fifties, who looks back on his life since the war and hates both it and himself. He is a third-generation academic, and the previous two generations of his family all spent their lives trying to avoid any sort of positive action, and above all keeping clear of politics. At the time of the 'Doctors' plot' in Stalin's last years, Ilya's father was implicated because one of the doctors was a close colleague of his. To avoid trouble, he resigned his job and decided to go and work in the far North – but he had a heart attack and died before he could get there. His son Ilya's trouble is his inability to say no – to his wife, his mistress, people who come to show him manuscripts of their war memoirs, or ask him to write a preface to a translation of a foreign historical novel, or beg him to get their relatives accepted as students at his institute. He married the wrong wife, Kira, whom his family all dislike; she is devoted to him, but she has no cultural background, thinks only of acquiring consumer goods and being seen with the right people, and tries to push her husband by force up the ladder of advancement. She wants him to apply for the job of Dean of his institute; but Ilya is a writer, not an administrator. As time goes by, he feels himself hopelessly trapped in a life of sham and lies.

In one scene of Baklanov's story, Ilya is travelling home on a trolleybus which is continually being overtaken by a lorry full of cattle going to the slaughterhouse. Every time they stop at traffic-lights, Ilya can see the cows' muzzles poking through the boards on the side of the lorry and their eyes staring at him. No one else seems to care about the animals' fate, and the woman sitting next to him has a shopping bag bulging with fat sausages. There are echoes of Pasternak in this story: Dr Zhivago's last moments, sitting in a hot Moscow tramcar and about to have a heart attack. Baklanov's hero also has a heart attack, but it is not a fatal one: there is to be no escape for him from his trapped existence, and he remains quite incapable of taking any practical step to alter his way of life.

Another source of pressure on Soviet intellectuals, and one much satirised, is the need to keep up with the Ivanovs. Baklanov's Ilya Konstantinovich is constantly pressurised by his wife to be polite to the right people and acquire material goods suitable to his station in life. Barely able to read or write, she feels that as the wife of a history professor she ought to fill their flat with antiques. One day she comes home delighted with a new purchase – an ornate mirror dating from the reign of Tsar Paul. Ilya reflects sourly to himself:

> She is the daughter of a floor-polisher. And her mother used to sit at a street crossroads with a big metal shovel, and change the points on the tram rails so that the trams could alter direction. It's a forgotten speciality nowadays, everything is done automatically now. But in those days, come rain or shine, there she would sit out there on a three-legged stool, with a shawl tied round her shoulders and a metal rod in her hands. A mirror from Paul I's reign – where on earth did my wife get that from? . . . She is intoxicated by the possibility of owning such an object, by the fact that her image is now reflected in this mirror, which once reflected scented, powdered ladies in Paul I's day – it makes her feel good . . . And she is a woman who never writes letters, because her handwriting is uneducated and she can't spell . . .

Kira in that story is depicted as an ignorant Soviet snob of the most objectionable kind, and there are many more examples of such types being satirised in recent fiction. People who buy books, not to read but to line their walls, are a frequent target for *feuilletons* in the press. As one journalist recently pointed out, 'People buy books in order to acquire prestige and become pseudo-intellectuals. Sportsmen and leading factory workers like to be interviewed and photographed against bookshelves containing works by Jack London, Vasili Belov, Marina Tsvetaeva.'[7] At its crudest this craving to own some rare commodity which your neighbours and friends do not possess can lead to scenes of vulgar showing-off. An elderly writer on agricultural topics, Ivan Vasiliev, described how he bought an overall one day in a town shop, and then wondered why the woman assistant was taking so long to wrap it up for him:

> Then I realised what she was doing: she was showing off her gold. On eight of her ten fingers she was wearing gold rings – some with stones, some without, some round, some oval, some lightweight and some really massive rings. Why ever did she have so many of them, I wondered. Her hands were well cared for, but dirty from the paper and string she was handling. I felt like asking her, Has no one taught you what bad taste is? – but she would have been offended, so I kept quiet. She'll learn better, in time. At the present moment she is simply drunk with her own success in getting hold of this gold which she is now showing off, and which makes her feel important.[8]

The most sought-after status symbol in all strata of Soviet society nowadays is the privately-owned car, and many novelists have described the lengths to which would-be motorists will go in order to outdistance their rivals and get a car quickly. Yuli Krelin, author of several popular stories about hospital life, set one of them in a small town near Moscow where a woman surgeon spends four days out of her annual holiday queueing up to put her name down for a new car.[9] This is at the end of the winter, and 1400 people queue day and night on a piece of waste ground outside town: the first hundred eventually succeed in getting their names registered – and then have to wait a further year before the new cars arrive.

Soviet snobbism can also take subtler forms which particularly affect the intelligentsia, who traditionally tend to live among small circles of acquaintances, meeting frequently and vying with one another in taking up the latest crazes fashionable in their particular group. A senior writer, Anatoli Ananiev, has satirised this tendency in his novel *The Years without War*, which appeared early in 1979.[10] Ananiev, who is editor of the hard-line journal *Oktyabr*, takes as his main characters a group of young Moscow intellectuals, mostly historians or journalists. They attend regular formal gatherings or soirées at each others' houses – and at these parties there is always someone who is being lionised, sometimes deservedly and sometimes not. For a time in the summer of 1966, so Ananiev relates, the guest of honour in this circle was a young 'unrecognised genius' from the provinces, named Nikitin. He was a post-graduate student from a provincial town, anxious to meet 'people in the right circles' who would help him to get his book published. The subject of this work was the Russian school of icon-painting: several publishers had turned it down on the grounds that it was merely a clumsy rehash of various authors' theories, but Nikitin liked to let it be thought that the reason for the repeated rejections was the extraordinary novelty and daring of his comments on medieval art. Gradually he built up for himself the reputation of a man being persecuted for his single-minded pursuit of the truth. And because he was wearing this halo of an undervalued genius – so Ananiev comments – he was a welcome guest in the homes of members of the sensation-starved Moscow literary fringe.

According to this same Ananiev novel, the really 'in' hobby among the young professional Moscow élite in the late 1960s was to keep a large pedigree dog. Ananiev gives a long description of a dog show held on the banks of the Moskva river on a summer Sunday, where the dog-owners range in occupation from ordinary workers to members of the Academy of Sciences. He tries to explain, with somewhat ponderous sarcasm, why these people have all been seized with such a passion for man's four-footed friends. A large part of their lives is devoted to the animals, and they justify this to themselves on the grounds that they are nature freaks. Keeping a large dog in a small Moscow flat (probably spending most of its time shut up in a stuffy room or kept out on a dusty balcony) means, so they maintain, that they have got regular contact with nature in the form of a living being sharing their home – and contact with nature, as is well known, renders the human heart better and nobler. But is this really the reason for the craze for large dogs, Ananiev asks?

In the opinion of some observers, all this love of nature conceals some quite different motives. Three times a day, winter and summer, the owners have to take their charges out for a walk to satisfy the needs of nature. And a man taking a well-groomed setter out on a lead resembles – even in the distance – a *barin* or nobleman. And although the packs of hounds for hunting, and the kennels where the noblemen used to keep them and which are so vividly described in Russian literature, have long since ceased to exist; although these noblemen's apartments, where big English or German dogs wandered around or lay on sofas next to their masters and were looked after by the servants – although all that has gone, that way of life with plenty of beautiful objects and dogs still has a great attraction for many people. The animals complicate their lives enormously: but it is well worth it to them, for the sake of those few minutes every day when they can appear in public with their well-groomed dog, and can feel themselves to some small extent a part of that old, noble way of life . . .

A few years after the big-dog craze, yoga hit Moscow. The hero of a story by Vasili Tishkov, which appeared in 1983,[11] describes his unsatisfactory life in town with a cranky wife, who won't cook meat for him although she feeds her poodle on liver sausage (of which the dog generously allows him a share):

She's studying yoga. That's a system for living, thought up by the ancient Indians. So now I've got my own Yoga in the house. She lives strictly according to a system . . . In the morning she drinks two litres of water on an empty stomach and eats some kind of mixture made out of grass. For lunch (she's at work by then) she has a carafe of tap water, a French loaf of bread and some coleslaw. In the evening, as soon as she gets back from work, she cooks up some vegetable broth from whatever she's managed to buy in the shops. And all this without any salt: that's very important. Before she goes to sleep, she sits down on a mat in the middle of the living-room, cross-legged in the Turkish fashion, and meditates for a couple of hours. That's how the yogas achieve Prana – what that is, I never could find out from her. Then she lies down to sleep on almost-bare boards, her arms by her sides; she goes all limp like a piece of macaroni, as though all the strength had gone out of her. Instead of 'Good-night' she usually says 'Don't touch me, I've switched off'. And believe it or not, she really looks switched-off, lying there like a corpse – even her face goes pale . . . I'm so afraid she may put the poodle on to the same system – then we shan't ever see any more liver sausage at home.

But the most galling pressure upon Soviet intellectuals is not the struggle to find material goods to spend their royalty fees on, nor yet the temptation to succumb to the latest fads of fashion, nor even the need to sell one's soul by denouncing a colleague so as to maintain one's own position. It is the constant pressure from editors, which has to be fought paragraph by paragraph and sentence by sentence in order that the author's work can be published in the form in which he wrote it. Not surprisingly, there are no explicit examples of the application of political censorship to be found in officially published Soviet fiction. But there is one scene in which an author's indignation at the revision of his scientific text is satirically described. This occurs in Alexander Kron's novel *Insomnia*[12] (for a scene of bribery from the same novel, see pages 66–7). The hero of the novel, Oleg Yudin, is a biologist working on problems of ageing. He has just come back from an official trip to Paris to attend a conference, and is working at home on his research, when one day he gets an unsolicited visitor to his Moscow flat. This is a pretty young girl reporter from a popular-science magazine, who has been sent round to get Yudin to look over the proofs of an interview which he gave some weeks earlier to one of her colleagues. He asks to see the original transcript of the interview, and finds it has been extensively edited, and a new title has been inserted: 'The Struggle against Death'. He protests that his work is nothing to do with preventing death, only with the study of premature ageing and what causes it. A long argument ensues, during which it becomes clear to Yudin that the magazine editors have trimmed his interview to fit in with the views of a fellow-scientist from his Institute, whom he knows to be a charlatan. This man, who enjoys official backing, has written an article stating that very soon scientists will discover how to double man's present life-span. Yudin next demands to see the proof-sheets of his interview, and these turn out to have been even more severely edited. He finally loses patience:

'No, dear lady: I won't sign this.'

'Why ever not?'

'Because it's not what I said.'

'Really, you are being tiresome. Some of it had to be edited. After all, they edited Chekhov and Tolstoy too . . .'

'My dear lady,' I said. 'Let's get quite clear what a magazine interview is. An interview – or so I have thought until now – is something arranged by a group of editors when they want to discover some specialist's personal opinion, expressed in his own individual way. If my views, and the form in which I am accustomed to expressing them, do not suit the editors; if they want to see their own views reflected in the interview – then they must abandon this genre, or else look for another victim.'

'So what's the solution?'

'Very simple: just print the interview as it was in the first place.'

Yudin is clearly bound to lose this argument, but he is determined to protest all the way. He picks out one of the many instances where what he told the interviewer has been altered by the magazine's editor. Asked which were his favourite composers, he had given a short list which included César Franck. But this name has now been removed from the list and replaced by Tchaikovsky. The girl reporter, who has obviously never heard of César Franck, hopes to pacify Yudin by promising to reinstate his name; but she refuses to remove Tchaikovsky, on the grounds that he is now in fashion because of the following year's Tchaikovsky competition in Moscow.

Yudin explodes. You aren't interested in what I really think, he cries – you just want the interview to be 'in the fashion'. He wants to withdraw the whole text and write a letter of protest to the magazine's editor. But the girl reporter now plays her trump card. If you do that, she says, they'll retire my colleague Yakov Semyonovich who took the original interview; they've been wanting to put him out on pension for a long time. Yudin remembers the interviewer: a middle-aged man, obviously Jewish, with a large family to support. He gives in, and signs the galley proofs.

REFERENCES

1 Galina Shergova, *Zakolochennye dachi* (*Novy Mir* 1978, no. 3).
2 Alexander Zinoviev, *The Radiant Future* (English translation), Bodley Head 1981.
3 Yuri Trifonov, *Vremya i mesto* (*Druzhba Narodov* 1981, nos. 9–10).
4 Fyodor Abramov, *Dom* (*Novy Mir* 1978, no. 12).
5 Valeri Chalidze, *Sakharov and the Russian Intelligentsia* (*Kontinent* 1981, no. 28).
6 Georgi Baklanov, *Men'shi sredi brat'yev* (*Druzhba Narodov* 1981, no. 6).
7 M. Levin, Article in *Zhurnalist* 1982, no. 1.
8 Ivan Vasiliev, *Zemlya russkaya* (*Nash Sovremennik* 1981, no. 12).
9 Yuli Krelin, *Svoi i chuzhye* (*Oktyabr* 1981, no. 4).
10 Anatoli Ananiev, *Gody bez voiny*, Part 2 (*Novy Mir* 1979, nos. 2–3).
11 Vasili Tishkov, *Vstrecha na rosstani* (*Yunost* 1983, nos. 4–5).
12 Alexander Kron, *Bessonitsa* (*Novy Mir* 1977, nos. 4–6).

6 New Views of Soviet History

Until recently, Soviet historians have usually given what seems to Western readers a very one-sided view of events in their country. Writers of Soviet historical novels have been even more categorical, dividing their characters into good Reds and bad Whites and leaving no shadow of doubt as to which are right. Just lately, however, some stories and novels in the official literary journals have been admitting that things were never that simple, and that terrorist acts were certainly committed by both sides. The hero of one recent novel, for instance, is an old man in his seventies looking back on his own role in the civil war. In 1919, he remembers, he was a boy of eighteen serving with a Red unit in southern Russia – and chairing a revolutionary tribunal with powers of life and death over hundreds of people. But how easily he might have found himself in the opposite camp, he thinks; and how wrong people are today, who oversimplify the past.

> This is what I don't understand: they are all made out to be black or white, devils or angels. And no one is in the middle. But everyone is in the middle. . . . What was I in August 1917? There was a general atmosphere of drunkenness, and I could have gone either way . . . People shouldn't lie about these things! Everyone's fate could have been quite a different one . . .

That was a passage from *The Old Man* by Yuri Trifonov.[1] In most of Trifonov's works the middle-aged or elderly heroes, living in present-day Moscow, look back at their own behaviour in the 1920s or 1930s and ask themselves whether they could have behaved differently: in particular, whether they could have done more to protect friends whose only crime was that quite by chance, they had found themselves on the losing side.

Yuri Trifonov himself was the son of an army officer who perished in the purges in 1938. In the civil war years Trifonov senior served with the Red Cossack forces in the Don area. Trifonov described his father's fate in an earlier novel, *The Campfire's Glow*, published in 1965. In his second novel, *The Old Man*, published in 1978, he took as the central figure his father's Cossack commanding officer, Mironov – changing his name to Migulin. The novel tells how in 1919 Migulin launched an offensive against Denikin's army in southern Russia without waiting for authorisation from the Red High Command. For this he was tried and sentenced to be shot by the Red Guards. He was pardoned that time, but perished two years later after he was again falsely denounced as a traitor: that time, they did shoot him. Trifonov makes it clear that Migulin was in fact devoted to the Communist cause, but that his Party bosses were suspicious of him because he was known to be a fiery Cossack patriot; they feared he was becoming a popular hero who might even have ended up as a Russian Garibaldi.

All these details correspond exactly with the known life of the real-life Cossack commander, Mironov. Interestingly enough, that biography can be checked from a contemporary Soviet source, the many-volumed *Great Soviet Encyclopedia.* Two editions of this work have been published since the war, with considerable variations between the first and second. In the 'M' volume of the 1954 edition there is no mention of a soldier Mironov: Stalin had only just died, and to the compilers of the *Encyclopedia* a Cossack commander shot by the Reds towards the end of the civil war was still very much a non-person. But twenty years later, in the 1974 edition, there he is: Filipp Kuzmich Mironov, 'Soviet military leader, member of the Communist Party in the last year of his life, arrested and pardoned in 1919, successfully led the Red cavalry against Wrangel's army in 1920, awarded two Soviet military medals, died in the spring of 1921'. No mention is made of the way he died. Trifonov, using his family connections, was able to dig further into the character of Mironov, or Migulin, and thus help complete the rehabilitation of his father's friend. In his novel he drew on reminiscences and diaries of people who knew Mironov well, and he also quoted from the official transcript of his trial to reconstruct the atmosphere of those stormy days.

Through the mixture of fact and fiction one can clearly feel Trifonov's own attitude: he has little sympathy with the black-and-white approach of the Red authorities of those days. The truth about Mironov/Migulin, in Trifonov's view, was that he was neither a villain nor a hero. He was a patriot who backed the Red cause, but was unable to go along with what was being done to his Cossack fellow-countrymen in the name of the revolution. The storyteller in this novel, the old man Pavel Letunov, makes the comment that Migulin lacked the necessary suppleness to survive in those grim days.

Letunov himself did not break: as a lad of eighteen, though he had a few doubts, he carried out without open protest the orders he received, about confiscation of grain and cattle and ruthless suppression of any Cossack opposition. Only after fifty years, looking back on his youth, is Letunov really horrified at some of the things he did:

> When you're in the midst of the lava stream, you don't notice the heat. . . . Some of us were horrified by the directives we got . . . But my God, how few people there were who protested their horror! The lava blinded their eyes, and it was hard to breathe in that crimson fog.

When his superior officer fell ill with typhus, Letunov (against his will) was appointed chairman of a revolutionary tribunal. Soon afterwards, the so-called Red Steel Brigade arrived in his area, headed by a wild extremist named Braslavsky; and Letunov found his duties included signing the orders for shooting hostages:

> I was eighteen, and in my hands were the lives of hundreds of peasants of whom I was afraid, women whom I did not know, and old men whom I did not understand . . . It was 1919, the Cossack communities were in revolt . . . and Braslavsky issued the order: 'Dig a common grave for the hostages' . . . And I had a terrible thought: Is Braslavsky in his right mind? Am I in my right mind?

He signs the death warrants; the hostages are shot, and a few weeks later the Steel Brigade leader Braslavsky is liquidated in his turn.

Towards the end of this novel, someone asks the now-old Letunov whether he feels any personal guilt about Migulin's death. After all, when Migulin was about to be tried the first time the investigator had asked Letunov if he believed that Migulin had been involved in a counter-revolutionary plot. At the time Letunov had said to the investigator: yes, it is possible. But at the age of seventy he seems to have forgotten that he ever testified against his friend:

> No, I don't feel any guilt towards him. But I do feel guilt towards everyone else, towards all of you today: guilt because I did not share the truth with you, but kept it to myself. For truth, I believe, is only of real value when it is available to everyone. If you keep it to yourself, hide it under a pillow, as Shylock hid his gold, then it's worth nothing. And that's why I feel guilty now: because I haven't enough time left to share the truth with everyone.

This thought is implicit not only in this novel, *The Old Man*, but in all Trifonov's books. He was always concerned with finding out the truth about the Soviet past; and a surprising amount of that truth did get published in his fiction.

Trifonov was one of the few official writers to admit in print that a lot of innocent people perished at the hands of the Red Guards. A much less daring writer, Mark Elenin, recently published a documentary novel about some of the White generals in the last days of the civil war. The book is called *Seven Deadly Sins*[2] and is set during the last months in the Crimea of Wrangel and his staff, before their evacuation in November 1920. Elenin uses quotations from official correspondence and army orders (taken mostly from memoirs which the White generals published abroad as émigrés) in order to reconstruct the struggle for power between Wrangel and the other generals; but the picture he paints of them is by no means all black, and his fictional heroes, the Belopolskys, members of a Liberal noble family, are sympathetically drawn. General Wrangel is shown as a cold, correct officer of the old school, whose worst fault is his vanity: he keeps a diary in which he embellishes reality and shows himself in the most favourable light, for the benefit of future historians. But he also displays courage, refusing to be evacuated until the last possible moment. Elenin describes the departure ceremony in Sevastopol:

> It was a sunny day. Wrangel went slowly up the steps to the Princes' Wharf, where a carefully-rehearsed performance awaited him. A band was playing. Troops marched past in parade order, the gold embroidery on the priests' robes catching the sun, sweet-smelling smoke rising up from their censers. A gaily-dressed crowd of spectators applauded their leader as he appeared, and flowers were thrown at his feet. He was well aware that things would not go on like this for much longer; and yet he was still hopeful, still confident of his own ability to accomplish what neither Kolchak nor Denikin had been able to do. The last six months had been a failure, he knew, and he asked himself where his mistakes had lain. Had he been insufficiently strict, or insufficiently liberal? Could anyone else in his place have done better? And what should he do now – abandon this army in which no one believed any more, or try to preserve it, revive its fighting spirit? . . . At this present moment, only one thing was important: he must conduct himself as befitted a commander-in-chief, a leader who was retreating for the time being in order to continue the struggle for a White victory . . . Wrangel slowly lowered himself on to one knee, picked up a handful of earth, kissed it and put it into a handkerchief . . . The launch cast off from the wharf and made its way out to the cruiser, the *Admiral Kornilov*.

Elenin never leaves his readers in any doubt that the White cause was doomed from the start, or that those who perished deserved their fate. But he treats the White refugees with considerable sympathy, giving a vivid description, for instance, of the crowds of women and old people in Sevastopol port, fighting to get aboard the fleet of over one hundred naval and merchant vessels – Russian, English, American and French – which transported thousands of them across the Black Sea to Constantinople and exile. Much of the novel is evidently based on memoirs of the time, most of them published in exile and not generally available to Russian readers. Only when he tries to draw moral conclusions is Elenin's story unconvincing. Thus at the end of a long passage describing conditions on board an old troopship, the *Nadezhda*, where the enormous crowd of assorted refugees are divided between cabins and the hold according to their social class, he gives a conversation between a White officer and an unknown fellow-passenger, in which the latter says what a good thing the Bolsheviks have done for Russia in clearing out all the dross and muck of the old Russian society and exporting it overseas. Most of the refugees, he indicates, have been guilty of all seven of the deadly sins and well deserve to be exiled. Oddly enough, this was one of the passages in the book which was lambasted by a Soviet critic. *Seven Deadly Sins* appeared in the Leningrad literary journal *Neva* early in 1981. A few months later the book was reviewed in another journal, *Nash Sovremennik,* where Elenin was sharply criticised for suggesting that it was only the bad element from the old Russia who fled abroad after the revolution. The critic Sergei Semanov reminded Elenin that those who left Russia after 1917 included many greatly respected names: Chaliapin, Rachmaninov, Anna Pavlova, Bunin and many others. According to Semanov, Elenin's novel gives an oversimplified and superficial account of important events, and I suppose this criticism is justified. But the book, although written in pedestrian style, is carefully documented and full of detailed information about historical personages who until now have hardly been mentioned in official history books. This novel, and Trifonov's *The Old Man*, are the first Soviet works I have come across since Sholokhov's *Quiet Flows the Don* in which a successful attempt is made to show what life must have been like for ordinary Russians who were not politically minded, but who were caught up in the turmoil of civil war. This is a period about which most young Russians know very little, unless they have grandfathers who can remember it.

Nor do they know much from official sources of the inside story of collectivisation – what life was like in the countryside in the early 1930s. For nearly thirty years there was no reference to this subject in official Soviet fiction. In 1964, at the end of the 'thaw' period under Khrushchev and eight months before he fell from power, *Novy Mir* published a story *On the Irtysh River* by a writer from Siberia, Sergei Zalygin.[3] It caused a sensation at the time because of its sympathetic portrayal of a peasant, Stepan Chauzov, who in 1931 was unjustly expelled from his local *kolkhoz* as a kulak.

In fact he was loyal to Soviet power; indeed, he had fought with the Red partisans against Kolchak's forces. His only crimes were that he had shown some reluctance over giving up his two horses when the local *kolkhoz* was formed, and that he had given shelter to the destitute wife and children of a neighbour who fled after burning down the collective's grain store. But these rather slender grounds for suspicion were enough to get Chauzov's name put on the list of peasants hostile to the new order. At the end of Zalygin's novel a Party official actually admits that Chauzov was not really a kulak at all; but he justifies the exiling of this man and his whole family by quoting the Russian saying: 'When you're felling the forest, the chips must fly' – a phrase one meets again and again in the official justifications of Stalinism.

Zalygin, who is now nearly seventy and currently writing a novel set in the 1920s, the period of the New Economic Policy, was one of the pioneers of the rustic school of 'village writers'. Later authors of this school have mostly set their stories in the war and post-war years, never in the 1930s when collectivisation first came to the villages. Now, however, a few revealing glimpses of those grim days are finding their way into officially published fiction. Some of the older writers seem to be anxious to get the more hideous events of their own childhood recorded in print before all the eyewitnesses die out.

Take Mikhail Alekseyev, now in his sixties and editor of the squarely conservative journal *Moskva.* His latest novel, *The Hotheads,* has been appearing in another conservative journal with a strongly nationalist profile, *Nash Sovremennik (Our Contemporary).*[4] The novel is frankly autobiographical, and gives a realistic, if limited, picture of collectivisation in a village in the Volga steppes. The story is told through two pairs of eyes, both belonging to the author. Alekseyev writes all the factual material from the viewpoint of his schoolboy hero, Mikhail; but from time to time he inserts a reflective passage in which Mikhail as an elderly man looks back at the events of the early 1930s and tries (rather half-heartedly) to find an explanation for them. The device works pretty well, and it gives two dimensions to a matter-of-fact account of a grim period of Soviet history. But Mikhail the boy emerges as much more sincere and believable than Mikhail the mature commentator. The boy is shown accepting the changes in his village, as any child would. In 1930 he goes to the meetings at which one-third of the peasant households are branded as kulaks, and he goes round with his schoolfellows in 'agitation brigades' organised by the schoolmaster, arguing with the remaining peasants and trying to persuade them to join the new collective farm. The boy does not witness any violence being applied: he sees the wooden boards with the word 'Boycott!' being nailed up on the gates of households on the new authorities' black list, he sees the farmhouses left empty when the alleged kulak families either flee or are deported, he sees the fires which keep breaking out all over the village – which some people say are the kulaks' revenge, but others that they are just the work of hooligans. And then we get flash-forward passages in which Mikhail as an old man points out that nothing very terrible in fact happened to these Volga kulaks. Some of them, he recalls, were exiled to distant parts of the USSR: one of them returned home to the village fifteen years later from Kazakhstan, to reveal that he had become chairman of a very wealthy *kolkhoz* out near Alma Ata. And soon after the end of the war Mikhail came across a small village on the opposite bank of the Volga, not far from Saratov, where a whole group of peasants from his home village had taken refuge in 1930. They had survived there for fifteen years undetected by the authorities, keeping their heads down, taking humble jobs on the Volga ferries or as nightwatchmen, and making a living by growing vegetables and catching fish to sell in the Saratov market.

These individual success stories may well have been drawn from real life, but Alekseyev clearly realises that just quoting these few cases is hardly enough to offset the thousands of deaths which resulted from the policy of collectivisation, and which many of his readers must still remember. The story of the novel continues through the terrible starvation winter of 1932–3. In his account of this through the boy Mikhail's eyes, Alekseyev does not spare the horrific details; and in his reflections put in the mouth of the old Mikhail, he makes a surprising admission. The Volga peasants, he writes, have always known that a summer of drought means a bad harvest, and that in turn means a hungry winter – as happened in his own experience in 1921. But in 1933 the peasants' hunger was not the result of natural causes:

> I must confess that I am still trying to work out the cause of this famine. The 1932 harvest was not the best ever, but it certainly wasn't a bad one. The *kolkhoz* workers in our village got 100 grams of grain per labour-day as an advance, and were looking forward to getting another kilogram per labour-day later on, when their accounts with the State were finally settled. But this hope foundered when suddenly a grain delivery plan was announced, and was carried out with unnecessary zeal by the local authorities and by uneducated activists. The very last grain of corn was gathered up, and the local people were left without bread and the *kolkhoz* horses without oats.

It has taken nearly fifty years before even this guarded admission that large numbers of peasants starved to death as a result of deliberate official policy could appear in a novel. Alekseyev is a sound establishment man, who has frequently declared that collectivisation was the correct policy for Russia, indeed that without it she could not have won the Second World War. The passage quoted above is immediately followed by one in which he pays tribute to the memory of his fellow-villagers who died during the 1933 famine. Right up to their last breath, he stresses, these men and women remained Soviet patriots, and they passed on their faith in Soviet power to the next generation, those who were children in 1933 but who were destined to fight for their motherland in the years that followed.

Alekseyev then goes on to describe just how his fellow-villagers died. He has published some earlier stories about famine in the countryside, based on autobiographical material: but some passages in this new novel are grimmer than anything he has written yet. His schoolboy hero sees the numbers of his classmates in the village school steadily dwindling through the winter. The family's old horse, which they handed over to the *kolkhoz,* gets thinner and weaker and finally dies. The boy's own family survives only because during the previous summer they had a good harvest of pumpkins from their private plot of ground. The worst time was the following March and April (1933), when there was snow still on the ground, hardly any animals were left, and those people who were still strong enough to move about wandered round the neighbouring villages searching for potatoes, or for some bran to mix with bits of vegetable peelings to make potato cakes. The children scoured the woods for roots and edible plants. Some of the men went to the quarry where the corpses of dead horses and cattle were thrown and cut bits off them; Alekseyev's boy-hero recognised the corpse of their own family horse with one leg missing. At the end of April things improved: corn sowing began, and those working in the fields gobbled handfuls of the seed corn; then the rooks returned and could be trapped, and there were fish in the streams. So the youngest and strongest survived into the summer; but the old and the weak were gone by then, leaving problems for their relatives who had to dig the graves. Alekseyev's storyteller recalls what happened when his grandfather died. Two bitter village enemies, Grigori and Petrukha, met at the graveside – one dead, the other still just alive.

> At the funeral, carts bearing dead bodies kept arriving from all directions, and people who hadn't the strength to dig even a shallow hole in the ground were begging my father for permission to inter their dead in grandfather's grave. The grave-diggers were just beginning to fill it in when Grigori's body was brought along by his sons. Room was found for this body too, wrapped as they all were in a cloth: it was placed in the top layer in the common grave. Uncle Petrukha, his face black as soot, drew a deep breath and said in a hoarse, barely audible voice: 'Well, there it is, Grigori. We were fools to spend so much time quarrelling. Maybe we'll end up lying side by side. What hotheads we were!' . . . It was only three days later that his sons Ivan and Yegor brought Uncle Petrukha's body to the cemetery. They dug up the top of grandfather's grave, and laid the coffinless body of their father alongside Grigori's, shoulder to shoulder . . .

Another theme from Soviet history which has been very seldom mentioned in works of literature is the sufferings of the Soviet Jews at the hands of the Germans during the last war; it has been almost totally ignored for nearly forty years. Published statistics give the total number of civilians killed during the occupation, but without specifying how many of them were Jewish; war memorials commemorating those killed by the Germans do not indicate the victims' nationality. At Babi Yar on the outskirts of Kiev, where the Germans murdered 95,000 Jews (and a great many Russians and Ukrainians), there is now a modest memorial on the site of the mass grave – but no reference appears on it to the fact that nearly all those who lie there were Jewish. Until very recently the only literary references to that tragedy were Yevgeni Yevtushenko's poem 'Babi Yar' published in 1961, and the first, censored, version of Anatoli Kuznetsov's documentary novel (also called simply *Babi Yar*) which appeared in the youth magazine *Yunost* in 1966.

In the last couple of years, however, this silence about the fate of the Jews has been occasionally broken. The monthly magazine *Teatr*, for instance, published a play by a well-known Ukrainian Jewish writer, Alexander Borshchagovsky.[5] Entitled *The Ladies' Tailor*, it is set in Kiev in September 1941 in a Jewish tailor's flat, on the night before all the Jews are due to assemble with their belongings. They have been told they are to be deported by train to Germany: in fact, they are massacred at Babi Yar. The characters in the play are old Isaac's Jewish family and a Russian family to whom the flat has been allocated by the occupying German authorities. During the night the two families, at first mutually suspicious, become friends. Isaac makes a tailored 'English' suit for the Russian granny, Evdokia, and the two thirteen-year-olds (one from each family) start a children's love affair. In the morning the Jewish family join the crowd of thousands of other Jews walking past the house on their way to their deaths.

The general theme of this play is Russian–Jewish friendship: old Isaac makes frequent remarks such as 'We're all people . . . Jews are just like other men – some are good, some bad'. The implication is that the various Soviet nationalities all live happily alongside one another, all treated equally by law. It's the official Party line, and Borshchagovsky is nowadays an official Party writer; in the last years of Stalin's reign he was accused of being a cosmopolitan and spent a short period under a cloud, but since then all his novels and plays have been full of Soviet, not Jewish, patriotism. *The Ladies' Tailor* is a very bad play, the characters all unbelievable and talking in stereotyped phrases, but it is one of the very few works of Soviet fiction which mentions the massacre at Babi Yar.

The theme of Russian–Jewish friendship is also basic to a novel by Anatoli Rybakov, *Heavy Sand*,[6] about the fortunes of a large Soviet Jewish family of shoemakers, living in a small town in the Western Ukraine between the years 1910 and 1942. The members of this family are shown as completely assimilated, loyal Soviet citizens, who were very seldom conscious that they were in fact Jewish – until the arrival of the Germans. Then they discovered what racial persecution meant. This book, as far as I know, contains the first official Soviet admission that the Germans set up as many as fifty Jewish ghettos on Soviet territory, and later exterminated the inmates when they were forced to retreat west.

Heavy Sand is a gripping story, available in English in a good translation. Rybakov is himself Jewish and comes from the western Ukraine, and though he has denied that the book is autobiographical, he has admitted gathering material for it from eyewitnesses, old people who remember what the Jews suffered. In the small town where the novel is located the Germans are shown forming a ghetto soon after their arrival in September 1941. A wire fence is put up to enclose the area: three main streets of the town with about 130 houses, into which 7000 Jews are crammed – 3000 inhabitants of the town, plus another 4000 from nearby towns and villages. Rybakov describes the Germans' deliberate policy of dehumanising the Jews, treating them like cattle. All who could work were made to labour twelve hours a day in the forest, tree-felling and transporting the timber; many of the Jews soon perished from overwork and starvation. Anyone suspected of links with the Russian partisans was mercilessly repressed: Rybakov describes in great detail the torturing to death of most of the members of his fictional family, including a teenage girl who was crucified and a child who was split in half with an axe. He also describes the steady growth of the will to resist among the desperate ghetto inhabitants. There is no mention of any Communists among these Jews, and no appeals were apparently made to their loyalty to the Soviet regime: they simply resolved to sell their lives as dearly as possible. The children stole weapons from the Germans and learnt how to use them, and at the end of the story, in the autumn of 1942 when the Germans decided to exterminate all the Jews that were left before they cleared out, there was an armed rising in this fictional ghetto. Six hundred of the more able-bodied broke out through the wire and joined up with the partisans in the forest. The Germans then liquidated the 2000 who were left behind, and razed to the ground the houses in the ghetto.

Rybakov ends the book with his storyteller, a member of the family who was away fighting at the front when these events took place, returning thirty years later to stand by the communal grave and read the inscription on the marble slab. On it is engraved in Russian: 'To the eternal memory of the victims of the German Fascist invaders'. Many real-life Soviet memorials have an identical inscription. But this fictional memorial also has some words in Hebrew: they actually come from the book of Joel. Rybakov quotes the Hebrew, and then translates it – 'Everything is forgiven, but those who have spilled innocent blood shall never be forgiven'. When first published in 1978 in the magazine *Oktyabr*, *Heavy Sand* took the Soviet reading public by surprise. The English translation of the book has not made nearly such an impact here, for we are quite accustomed to accounts of Nazi atrocities. But to Soviet Jewish readers this was a long-overdue tribute to the sufferings of their families, and the first public acknowledgement that the fate of the Jews was actually much worse than that of Russians or Ukrainians in the occupied territories. It is also a good example of recent works of fiction which give a fuller and more truthful picture of the Soviet past.

REFERENCES

1 Yuri Trifonov, *Starik* (*Druzhba Narodov* 1978, no. 3).
2 Mark Elenin, *Sem' smertnykh grekhov* (*Neva* 1981, nos. 1–3).
3 Sergei Zalygin, *Na Irtyshe* (*Novy Mir* 1964, no. 2).
4 Mikhail Alekseyev, *Drachuny* (*Nash Sovremennik* 1981, nos. 7 & 9).
5 Alexander Borshchagovsky, *Damski Portnoi* (*Teatr* 1980, no. 10).
6 Anatoli Rybakov, *Tyazhelyi pesok* (*Oktyabr* 1978, nos. 7–9). (English translation published Allen Lane 1981.)

7 Nostalgia for Old Russia

Plenty of Soviet citizens are dissatisfied with life. Those of them who are politically minded have gloomy discussions with their friends about the regime, and may go on to become open dissidents or even try to emigrate to the West. But a large proportion of discontented Soviet citizens are discontented for reasons very similar to those of thousands of people in other European countries. The roads are getting too crowded; the forests are being cut down; the lakes and rivers are polluted; no one bothers to make their own bread nowadays; people eat too much tinned food; no one knows how to harness a horse correctly, or how to carve the old designs on the wooden lintels, or work the old embroidery patterns, or sing the old songs. And the malcontents who complain about these things which are fast vanishing from modern Soviet life are increasingly spending their leisure digging up the pre-Revolutionary, mainly rural Russian past. These are the people who collect sleigh bells and bits of bridles to hang on the walls of small Moscow flats, and they are the members of the Russian Society for Preservation of Ancient Monuments, founded eighteen years ago with a membership of nearly a million, which has grown to more than twelve million since then.

One of the most active members of that society is the writer Vladimir Soloukhin, a lyrical poet and prose-writer, best known in England for his book about collecting icons, which has been published in translation. Soloukhin has done a lot to save many old church buildings from decay in various parts of Central Russia. Some time ago he wrote a long article for the journal *Moskva* drawing attention to the sorry state of a famous monastery which figures in several Russian classics.[1] The monastery is Optina, the setting for some of the best-known episodes in *The Brothers*

Karamazov. Not only Dostoyevsky but also Gogol and Tolstoy visited Optina to talk to the elders or holy men there. Soloukhin gives a detailed history of the monastery, founded in the days of Boris Godunov. In the nineteenth century it became a centre of the Slavophil, nationalist movement. Thousands of pilgrims made their way there in the years before the Revolution, and Soloukhin, realising that his contemporary Soviet readers might wonder what brought so many people to sit at the feet of the elders, gives an explanation full of his own longing for the old Russia:

> You have to imagine to yourself Russia as she was in those days, with all the complexity of social relationships between the various spheres of Russian life – between peasants, merchants, nobles, officials, priests. You have to imagine a Russia where there were hundreds of thousands of churches, thousands of monasteries, where people would have big celebrations for the saints'-day feasts, for weddings and funerals; a Russia where most people read very little, or could not read at all. And at the same time, this was a Russia whose people were longing to have their say, to speak out – and equally longing to hear some words of guidance, instruction and comfort. The elder was a holy man whose fame had spread all over Russia; you saw him only once in your lifetime, and so you could tell him everything, open your soul to him. And the people's faith in the elder's wisdom and perspicacity was limitless.

According to Soloukhin, there are still pilgrims of a sort going to Optina, for when he visited the monastery he found a coachload of tourists there. But there are no monks or elders left; the monastery walls are crumbling, and the churches are mostly roofless, except for those which have been patched up and are being used for secular purposes. After the Revolution Optina became a rest-home for a time; later it housed the offices of a state farm; now it is an agricultural trade school. Soloukhin comments that children should go to school in modern buildings with big classrooms, dry and warm, with plenty of light – not in an old cathedral whose roof lets the rain in. As for the graveyard, where it is known that seven of the most famous elders were buried (including the real-life prototype for Alyosha Karamazov's teacher, Father Zosima), as well as Tolstoy's aunt and the two Kireyevsky brothers (the first Slavophils) – Soloukhin writes that no one knows now which grave is which. Some years ago the marble headstones were found to have been torn up and scattered all over the monastery grounds. On the day Soloukhin was there the tourists at Optina heard an address at the cemetery, delivered by their guide, the curator of a local museum:

> The concept of the Motherland . . . is formed out of concrete things – peasant huts, villages, rivers, songs, stories, the beauty of architecture and landscape . . . So let us gather up and preserve, crumb by crumb and stone by stone, all these things which we can love and on which we can build our love of our native land.

Echoing the museum curator's appeal, Soloukhin called his article about the Optina monastery *A Time for Collecting Stones*. He ended with a plea for the restoration of all the one thousand known Russian monasteries, plus the tens of thousands of churches and country-house estates.

Another writer who is fascinated by the pre-Revolutionary Russian past is Vasili Belov. He has been avidly collecting old peasant customs, songs and sayings, and writing them down before they should be forgotten and lost. Belov was born in a village in the Vologda region, and he has recently written a series of essays on the old life in Northern Russia, which he can just remember from his own childhood (he is now in his fifties). The essays, entitled *Harmony: Essays in popular Aesthetics*,[2] appeared in the nationalist monthly, *Nash Sovremennik*.

Belov bases the title of his book on his belief that the old life in the Russian countryside was essentially harmonious, in tune with the world of nature. Everything went in cycles: a cycle for the summer and one for the winter, and indeed a lifelong cycle lasting from each man's conception until the grass was growing over his grave. He then gives a detailed description of the various occupations which were appropriate to the four seasons of the year. He lists the masters of many old village crafts which are fast dying out nowadays: shoemakers and stove-builders, horse doctors and millers, charcoal-burners and barrel-makers and wheelwrights.

He includes among these respected professional people the wise-women or sorcerers who could mix you a love potion or find your stolen goods, the women mourners who went round to wail at funerals, and the church bell-ringers. He has a whole chapter on the old Russian beggars, who were also members of an honoured profession. In the village community or *mir*, it was considered a great sin not to give alms to a beggar or to refuse him a free night's lodging. Very few beggars were deliberate layabouts according to Belov: they were usually the victims of fires or other catastrophes, whom the *mir* would help to get back on their feet again. Food and lodging would always be provided for travellers in distress, such as victims of highway robbery, or soldiers returning home on foot after serving out their twenty years in the army, or pilgrims on their way back from worshipping at a shrine. Cripples and blind men were held in special regard, being passed on from village to village and paying for their night's lodging perhaps by telling stories or singing ballads. Belov recalls one beggar, half-blind Vasya Chernyaev, who used to go round the villages in the Kharovsk district of Vologda province fifty or so years ago. He would knock on doors to beg for alms, and then recite a prayer calling on the Holy Spirit to protect a house and its inhabitants from the sword, bullets, fire, plague and robbers. Then he would make up his own improvised, rhyming stories about local, mostly comic events, and with these he would entertain the village children and ease his own conscience for accepting the alms which had been freely given him.

Vasili Belov writes at length about the old peasant craftsmen's love of their work. Money meant little to them and the best artists among them remained anonymous. Nowadays, Belov comments sadly, art objects are mass-produced, and book-keepers and economists keep totting up the costs and emphasising the need for quantity rather than quality. Modern lace, for instance, is produced by machines by the metre; but in the old days the women lace-makers made their kerchiefs for themselves or as presents – not for sale. As for the artists who did carvings in walrus-bone, or the painters of icons or of church frescoes, they had a very serious approach to their work, and would sometimes go into a period of rigorous training before embarking on an important project. Before starting work, the artist would go to the bathhouse, would fast, purify himself from all that was trivial – preparing himself for an inner explosion of creative imagination. The painter Andrei Rublyov, before starting his masterpiece 'The Trinity', fasted for forty days. Only in this frame of mind would a man receive that special and unexpected illumination when a work of art would form itself under his hands.

It is hard to accept Belov's essays as a rounded portrayal of the Russian past: surely, one feels, he must be romanticising it. He hardly mentions hunger or cold: according to him, the grim northern winters were enlivened by beer feasts, mummers at Christmas, young people's informal parties every night. Moral standards were high, and it was almost unheard of for a girl to have to get married. Even illiteracy, which he admits was universal in the old Russian village, is seen by Belov as having its positive side: for it was just because hardly anyone could read that story-telling became developed to a high art. But he gives a very charming picture of many aspects of the old life: for instance, the relationship between the peasant and his animals:

> The peasant always considered himself a part of nature. And the domestic animals were like a link between man and the huge and threatening forces of nature; his closeness to these animals softened the chill of loneliness which he felt when he gazed at the distant Milky Way . . . Horses were always given individual names . . . But the cows too had names . . . The mistress of the household would talk to them as though they were human, and the cows would respond with a deep moo, or by licking her or twitching their big, hairy ears. Calves, dogs and cats all had their own names . . .

Belov is rather careful not to deal with the peasants' attitude towards official religion, although he does pay tribute to the Orthodox Church for instilling in people (through its beautiful religious services) a love of painting, music and words. He describes at some length all the lay ceremonies connected with weddings, funerals and christenings, and also reflects on the peasants' superstitious beliefs. According to him, they did not make a clear distinction between reality and fantasy: traditional beliefs were mixed up with real happenings in the peasants' minds. No one would be so rash as to say firmly, 'There's no such thing.' People preferred the evasive formula, 'Who knows, perhaps it exists, perhaps it doesn't.' People who declared that they believed in nothing supernatural would be laughed at, even regarded as mental defectives. And almost everyone believed in the existence of house-spirits.

The house-spirit was known affectionately as the *domovushko*, and he was the protector and master of the house . . . He was almost a member of the family, like the horse or the cow. Sometimes he got angry and broke things, or he might leave the house for a time – in the latter event, misfortunes would happen one after another in that household. Outside in the stockyard, the guardian spirit was known as the *dvorovushko* . . . When leaving home for a long period – for instance before going away to work at hauling the river barges, or before reporting for military service – some peasants would go out to the barn and address the guardian spirit aloud, asking him to look after the yard and the animals in their absence. A kindly *dvorovushko* would sometimes reply by rustling with a broom or giving a light squeak or cough, just to reassure the master of the house that all would be well while he was away.

Vasili Belov looks at the Russian peasant's superstitious beliefs with a kindly smile, obviously reckoning that these customs dating back to pre-Revolutionary times are now just old men's tales. But are the old superstitions really quite dead? Not, it seems, if you look at a recent story by one of Belov's fellow-writers from the 'country' school, Fyodor Abramov. Called *Mamonikha* – the name of a small village in the northern forest – this story appeared in the Leningrad literary journal, *Neva*.[3] Its theme is one which was very dear to Abramov's heart: the closing down of hundreds of small villages, and the removal of their inhabitants to larger settlements, where they are put into modern flats with no land and no chance to keep animals. Abramov was in favour of the preservation of many of the smaller villages, both as a way of retaining the peasants' links with the land and preventing the neglect of outlying fields, and also as a means to the good life for country dwellers, which he saw as only possible in close contact with nature. The hero of this particular story is a townsman, Klavdi Ivanovich, who goes back to Mamonikha one summer with his wife and child, to spend a holiday camping out in his family's old house there. But his parents are dead and the village has been closed down: the street is overgrown with grass, the orchards and vegetable plots are a wilderness, the roof of the old house leaks – and there is only one permanent inhabitant left. This is old Granny Sokha who used to be much respected, and indeed feared, as the local wise-woman. During the holiday Klavdi Ivanovich's small son Viktor suddenly gets a bad attack of asthma. There is no doctor for many miles, so Klavdi fetches old Sokha to see if she can help the child. She begins by laying on hands and saying a prayer; but then she goes on to chant a rhyming spell over the sick boy. The words are very old and pagan, quite different from modern Russian speech:

> 'Ispolokhi, perepolokhi, porchi, uroki, vsyakie prikosy: Idite v penie, v korenie, v gryazi topuchi, v klyuchi kipuchi.
> Tam vam varitsya, tam vam kipyatitsya, pod osinovyi kol uiti;
> Kamnem nakrytsya, zemlyoi zavalitsya, mokhom-travoi zarasti . . .

('Out, out, leave him, all you fits and seizures: free him from all spells and from the evil eye. Out, out, into the stump of the tree, into the roots, deep down into the mud, into the bubbling spring. There may you boil, there may you seethe, down below the stake of aspen wood, underneath the stone, far beneath the earth – and may the grass and moss grow over you . . .')

Three times Sokha read the spell, three times she cursed all ills and pains, passing her hand lightly over Viktor's throat and chest – and already the child seemed to be wheezing less painfully, no longer gasping for breath. 'D-r-rink,' he said suddenly in a faint voice, and Polina gave him a drink.

'Now,' said old Sokha, 'now you, the father, must go outside and cut an aspen stake the length of an axe, and bury it deep in the earth, together with all the child's pains and ills. And no one must ever dig that stake up again.'

Klavdi Ivanovich does what he is told, although worried that some kind of black magic is involved. And when he comes back into the house, the child is obviously out of danger, the attack over. Very likely this whole incident got into the story simply because Abramov came across the spell and was fascinated by the old wording. But there it is, in a story by a contemporary Soviet writer: a child whose asthma had been treated by doctors without much success, miraculously cured by an old wise-woman's spell. There is no suggestion, of course, that the child's parents would ever resort to old Sokha's black magic again: the story ends with the family returning to the city, and the old woman is left alone in the abandoned village.

Writers like Soloukhin, Belov, Abramov are obsessed with the old Russian countryside and want to save as much of it as they can. But nostalgia for the pre-Revolutionary past can also affect writers whose novels have strictly urban settings, and whose heroes are engineers or scientists or civil servants. A recent example is the well-known novelist Daniil Granin (now in his sixties), whose latest novel, *The Picture*,[4] is full of nostalgia for life in a small Russian provincial town in the last century.

Granin's hero is Sergei Losev, mayor of the town of Lykov and an honest, patriotic local official, who boasts proudly of his new housing schemes and the maternity hospital he has just had built. He is, in fact, at the start of the story a very dull, careerist civil servant. But then something happens which changes his life. He goes to Moscow on business, and while he is there drops into an art exhibition, where his attention is riveted by a painting of a familiar view from his home town. It shows the old house built by a former timber-merchant, seen across a quiet stretch of the river. Losev gazes at the picture and memories of his own childhood, when he used to bathe in the river just there, come flooding back. He persuades the artist's widow to give him the picture, and takes it back to Lykov, where it arouses a lot of interest – the artist who painted it, long out of favour because he was too influenced by the French Impressionists, has just been rediscovered and is now much written about. His painting of the Lykov scene starts Losev off on a journey back into the past. He wonders what life in the town was like a hundred years ago when that timber-merchant's house was built. He goes to see an old retired official, Polivanov, now an amateur local historian; and there he is shown some old blueprints of pre-Revolutionary town-planning proposals. This town which was never built strikes him by its old-world charm: he unfolds the long rolls of paper and gazes at the houses and at the little illustrative drawings of carriages with horses and ladies with lace parasols. And he realises that although the old, pre-Revolutionary Lykov had obvious drawbacks (as he was continually pointing out in his official speeches) such as drinking dens, hovels for the workers, constant fires and epidemics, and of course no mains water supply – all the same, the old Lykov had also had proportions, elegance and quite a lot of comfort. The men who drew up those old blueprints had dreamt of and planned for a new Lykov in the future – just as he is doing today, he thinks. And he finds himself agreeing with the old amateur historian, Polivanov, when he tells him:

> 'We like to think that in the old Russia nothing was any good, everything was bad, it was just misery, oppression, savagery . . . We should have more respect for our ancestors!'

Losev soon finds himself in deep trouble in Granin's novel, because the view shown in the picture has been officially approved as the site of a new computer factory and the old merchant's house is due to be demolished. A local pressure group develops around old Polivanov, campaigning for the preservation of the house as a local museum and the river-bank as a public park. The most active member of the group is a guitar-playing young factory worker, Kostik. At nineteen he likes to wear worn jeans, an orange T-shirt with English slogans printed on it, and copper bracelets on his arms. He has a punch-up with one of the surveyors at the future factory-site near the old house, refusing to allow a tree to be cut down. Later on, the group's leader, old Polivanov, dies while making a protest march to the site. There is a twist in Granin's story here: for old Polivanov, who ends his life fighting to preserve one of the town's old buildings, had played a very different role when he was a militant Commissar in the 1920s. Then, he had headed the local firebrands who closed down the fourteenth-century Church of St Vladimir, looted its contents, and had an anti-religious bonfire outside in the main town square, where the iconastasis, many of the icons and most of the library of seventeenth-century religious books were all consumed. Thirty years later, in the 1950s, Polivanov became interested in local history, and then he called on all the old women believers in Lykov, begging them to give him any of the icons and books they had managed to save from the bonfire. Most of the old women cursed him, but some forgave him and gave him a few surviving relics, which he kept carefully for posterity.

Losev's nostalgia for the past continues to dominate his life, getting in the way of his career. He argues too much with his superiors, and finally has to leave Lykov for an inferior job elsewhere. But he does manage to save the old house in the picture. Another site is found for the computer factory, and a few years later the house becomes the town museum, with the young protester Kostik as director.

An interesting postscript to this novel appeared in the weekly *Literaturnaya Gazeta*, showing what a very direct relation the story has to real Soviet life. The paper published the transcript of a conversation between the author, Granin, and the mayor of a small provincial town, Maloyaroslavets. Like the fictional town of Lykov, Maloyaroslavets is a centre for light industry; but it was originally founded in the fourteenth century, and still has a few old buildings left, notably a monastery which has been partially restored. The mayor's main problem, just as Losev's was in Granin's novel, is how to provide enough new housing quickly without spoiling the character of an old town. And while the fictional Losev looked admiringly at the old blueprints for nineteenth-century workers' cottages and contrasted them mentally with the ugly, prefabricated blocks of flats for whose construction he had been responsible, so the real-life mayor was advised by Granin to keep the old buildings, and as for new housing, 'let people build their own individual houses with gardens; that way you can best preserve the character of an old Russian provincial town'. If this can really be done, some Soviet citizens at least will get an opportunity to clothe their nostalgia in modern dress.

REFERENCES

1 Vladimir Soloukhin, *Vremya sobirat' kamni* (*Moskva* 1980, no. 2).
2 Vasili Belov, *Lad: Ocherki o narodnoi estetike* (*Nash Sovremennik* 1979, no. 10 & 1981, no. 1).
3 Fyodor Abramov, *Mamonikha* (*Neva* 1980, no. 9).
4 Daniil Granin, *Kartina* (*Novy Mir* 1980, nos. 1–2).

8 Writers and Religion

It is extremely hard to estimate the strength of religion in the Soviet Union: figures for church attendance and baptisms are not available, and any evaluation is mostly guesswork. Yet plenty of evidence of a widespread interest exists in works of fiction, despite the censorship to which they are subject. If confirmation is needed it can be found in Konstantin Chernenko's speech to the Party Central Committee Plenum in June 1983, in which he criticised writers, theatres and film studios for portraying unhappy and unstable heroes rather than positive characters – and added that there were too many examples of 'God-seeking motives' in contemporary works of art.

One Soviet writer who has lately been revealing a fascination with religious themes is the senior Party author, Daniil Granin. He included in his latest novel, *The Picture*[1] (see also pp. 129–31 above), this scene where the hero, a local official and a Party member, goes into a church with his girl-friend and finds a service in progress:

> It was the first time Losev had been inside a big, working church while a service was going on . . . The proceedings at the altar – the appearances and disappearances of the white-clad servers, the deacon swinging his censer, the procession of young priests in their brocade robes – it all seemed vaguely familiar, and he began remembering words he had never used and did not even know he knew . . . The choir started up: their resigned, melancholy voices rose up to the high dome, floated away into the blue ceiling with its painted angels and clouds. He seemed to have heard the simple melody before: it moved him, as one is moved by a dim memory of something left behind long

> ago ... The voices rose even higher, not complaining or lamenting, but carried high above the earth and its transitoriness; and the voices were full of hope, even though an illusory one. There must be something in all this, he thought: in the smoky, gilded faces on the icons, in the resonance within the dome, in one's reflections about the shortness of life here on earth and about what is to follow that life. Heavens above, do these people really believe? he asked himself, and answered – no, they are just hoping, not believing; there's nothing beyond the grave, we all know that. But his thoughts were confused, unfamiliar; he thought about how quickly his life was passing, how good it would be to live more slowly, and to do that one needed moments like this, in which to throw off everyday cares and look around one ...

Deeply impressed though he has been with the service, Losev is still fighting back, determined not to give in to the emotional pull of beautiful music backed by Russian historical tradition. But his schoolteacher girl-friend Tanya is not so tough, and seems to be on the brink of belief: she even admits to him that she was praying along with the congregation – although what to, she does not know.

After the service Losev and Tanya have a long conversation with one of the servers, a would-be priest who is at present doing penance for heresy. He maintains that the way to religious faith lies through doubts, and recommends them to read the Book of Job, about a man who asked God questions and, by so doing, got nearer to the ultimate truth. There are several references to Job in this novel: he seems to represent for Granin (whose first books were about scientists or engineers) the image of the first scientist or philosopher. In an article for *Oktyabr* about his views on literature, Granin stated that its highest function – like that of religion – is to ask questions rather than give answers:[2]

> Many people nowadays don't understand the meaning or the Biblical significance of the details in works of art which were painted on religious themes. Then how is it that these pictures still influence people? Is it just through the skill of those old painters? Or is it because these paintings reveal to us the road

which was followed by those artists in approaching the great questions about the purpose of suffering, about justice, faith, the forces of good and evil? A road which led them to questions, not to answers?

Another writer who has always posed questions for the reader to answer for himself is Vladimir Tendryakov. I have already dealt with two of his stories on problems of young people (see pp. 47–8 above). In all his works he raises moral issues, and often he shows his characters seeking guidance from religion. Since Tendryakov is a firm supporter of Soviet ideology, the religious answer usually fails to satisfy his seekers after truth; but nor are they content with stereotyped formulas for the meaning and aims of life. Tendryakov's own attitude towards religion, as far as one can judge from his stories, has progressed over the last twenty-five years from certainty that religion can only appeal to the most ignorant elements in Soviet society, to a state of complete bewilderment that it should still exist, more than sixty years after the Revolution, and still be influencing a minority of Soviet citizens. This progression can be clearly seen if we look at three of Tendryakov's stories, published in 1958, 1969 and 1977.

In *The Miraculous Icon*[3] a twelve-year-old village boy, Rod'ka Gulyaev, while fishing in the river, finds a box containing a miracle-working icon, which a believer had saved and hidden when the local church was closed, nearly thirty years earlier. Rod'ka has no father; he lives with his mother and grandmother, who are believers. The discovery of the icon provokes an explosion of religious fervour of the most ignorant and superstitious nature from the grandmother, and the mother is completely under her thumb and powerless to protect the boy. Her grandson was led by God to find the icon, the old woman declares, and he must now behave in a fitting manner. She beats Rod'ka until he submits to wearing a cross round his neck, and won't give him any food until he crosses himself and says a prayer to the icon. Her equally superstitious old cronies move into the house and bring with them cripples or sick folk who beg Rod'ka to put their petitions to the icon, and he is made to miss school. In the end his life becomes such a nightmare that the boy runs away from home and tries to drown himself, but is fortunately saved by the schoolmistress and the local *kolkhoz* chairman. This argument between the schoolmistress and the local priest seems to embody the author's own attitude in the late 1950s:

> 'By your insistence on the constant interference of God in men's lives, you are taking away man's right to order his life for himself.'
>
> 'What do you mean, we are taking away his right? By all means let people plough the earth, build factories, beget children, and live in fear of God the great and the just, Who will not allow evil to triumph.'
>
> 'You said – live in fear. Why do you think men need to live under the threat of a moral whip? Why do you think men can only be made to do good deeds out of fear of some kind of all-powerful force, not because they are capable of understanding the necessity for good deeds and the harmfulness of bad deeds? I am a teacher, and I know you cannot teach children through intimidation . . . I taught Varvara Gulyaev [Rod'ka's mother] to understand and think out everything for herself; I wanted her to become a human being with a broad outlook and with a reasoned faith in the future. But during the war years you imposed on her your faith – a blind faith, which does away with the need to think or reason. And the world became a dark place which she could not understand . . . Since the war life in this *kolkhoz* has got harder. How can things be improved? Your answer is: it's God's will . . . And from this spiritual blindness, from lack of knowledge, springs an animal fear of life – fear of God's wrath, fear of the bosses, fear of unseasonable rain, fear of a cat seen crossing the road . . . You have made men spiritually impoverished, turned them into moral cripples . . .'

The story ends with the schoolteacher taking Rod'ka to live with her, while the local Party boss expresses his confidence that, as the standard of life rises, so the number of believers will drop.

In *On Apostolic Business*, however, written in 1969,[4] this materialist philosophy is acknowledged as having failed to defeat religion. The hero, Yuri Rylnikov, is a young scientist with a family and a comfortable Moscow life. But he is tormented by the eternal questions – what is my place in the universe? Why was I born?

What is truth? How lucky, he groans, are those people for whom everything is clear: 'God has not knocked at their door'. God has knocked at Yuri's door so persistently that he buys a copy of the Bible, recites the Lord's prayer, decides that he is a believer, and then drops out of society. He spends some months in a remote Siberian village, working on the *kolkhoz* and lodging with an illiterate old woman believer. But he soon has conflicts both with the local officials and with the Christians – notably with old 'Sister Annushka'. She is a narrow-minded bigot; she has spent time in prison for her religious beliefs, but they are entirely negative and she has a fierce hatred of anyone educated, who thinks for himself. There is a young priest, Father Vladimir; but Yuri falls out with him too, after admitting that, unlike the priest, he does not believe every word of the Bible. Yuri accepts 'Love your enemies' but cannot accept Christ's miracles, and rebels against 'Blessed are the poor in spirit' – 'how can Christ prefer idiots to normal people?' he cries with a scientist's arrogance. Father Vladimir says Yuri is not a true believer: he only wants to believe, and he risks the eternal torture of Tantalus – to thirst in vain for the living water of faith. Then Yuri gets into arguments with his fellow workers and with the *kolkhoz* chairman, trying to prove to them that belief in God does not necessarily work against the building of communism, that there can be a spiritual as well as a material form of communism. But when he goes on to argue that some sort of immortality of the soul exists, the local officials lose all patience with him: they are afraid he will spread his belief in God among the villagers, and they tell him to go back to Moscow. He gets on the train to go home, having found no soul-mates during his apostolic sojourn in the village, but taking back with him a somewhat deeper understanding of the purpose of life:

> I have created a theory for myself. If God exists, then a higher, ultimate goal of life also exists. God Himself is unattainable, and God's goal cannot be comprehended by man's feeble reason; it is necessary simply to believe in that goal, as mathematicians believe that only one direct line can be drawn between two points on a flat surface. There is a Supreme Goal, the same goal for everyone! Believe in it, and strive towards it.

Harmony betwixt men, their love one for another – this is God's reflection, His shadow . . . Love thy neighbour!

This belief in the power of brotherly love crops up again in Tendryakov's writing eight years later, in the story *The Eclipse*[5] (see also p. 47 above). One of the main characters is a bearded drop-out, Gosha Chugunov, who rejects Soviet society and lives on charity. The hero of the story, a conformist young man named Pavel Krokhalev, meets Gosha in a railway station restaurant, where Gosha asks him for the price of a meal, and this conversation ensues:

'Who are you, you strange fellow?'

'Is it so strange not to have any money?'

'Not to have enough for a bowl of soup, yes. Nowadays everyone earns enough for that.'

'But I don't work.'

'What do you do, then?'

'I travel around, looking at things.'

'With any particular aim in view?'

'No.'

'But you must need money to travel about.'

'People give me money.'

'Who does?'

'Casual acquaintances like yourself.'

'They *give* you money? Voluntarily?'

'Don't worry, I'm not a robber or an extortionist . . .'

'But what happens if a stranger like myself turns out to be mean and won't give you money?'

'Then I'd find someone else – no problem. Haven't you noticed, there are a great many good people in the world – far more than there are hard-hearted people?'

'You seem to be an educated person – what training have you had?'

'I was at an economics institute, but I left in the fourth year.'

'Why?'

'Because I realised I was being trained up to take orders from somebody and to make other people obey me, and I don't want either of those things. I decided to live free from everyone and everything, to depend just on the kindness of people I meet . . . People very much want someone to accept kindness from them.'

Pavel does not accept Gosha's philosophy, regarding him at best as a peaceful anarchist and at worst as a parasite on society. But he gives him free lodging for a time in his flat, and Tendryakov devotes many pages of his story to the fruitless arguments between these two (equally fleshless and improbable) characters. Pavel believes in the power of science to transform the world; Gosha believes that, to be happy, men need a unifying belief in God through which they will gain spiritual brotherhood.

Pavel points out that in countries such as Italy where the population believe in God, brotherly unity is not particularly noticeable. But his wife Maya accepts Gosha's arguments, and takes Pavel to a Sunday afternoon prayer meeting in a private flat. A group of people of all ages sit round drinking tea, and one of the women, 'Sister Anfisa', sings a Psalm: 'The sorrows of death compassed me, and the pains of hell got hold upon me; I found trouble and sorrow.' Then Gosha addresses the gathering with his gospel of love. Afterwards Pavel and Maya continue the argument. Pavel objects that too much love can do people harm, not good: look at all those mothers who completely ruin their sons' characters by spoiling them. Maya sees Gosha as a modern Don Quixote, pure in heart and pursuing lofty ideals. Pavel comments sourly that Don Quixote in fact made things worse, not better: when he freed the prison chain-gang, for instance, all that happened was that the prisoners promptly beat him up and went off to commit more crimes. Pavel loses all the arguments; Maya leaves him and goes to live with Gosha – although Tendryakov makes it pretty clear that he does not give much for her chances of living happily ever after with this anti-social element.

In the description of Gosha's prayer-meeting congregation there are echoes of the explanation Tendryakov gave for the popularity of religion in his early story about the miraculous icon: most believers, he seems to be saying, are people who have suffered much in life, often women without men, lonely and unloved. But he is honest enough in *The Eclipse* to give us a God-seeking heroine who is young and beautiful and has an adoring husband.

Yet his explanation of why such a girl should feel the need for God – it is hinted in the story that her husband was too interested in material possessions, and that the young couple kept themselves to themselves too much, and so became alienated from Soviet society – lacks conviction. Pavel reflects on the fact that his love affair with Maya began during one eclipse of the moon and ended six months later with another, and consoles himself with the thought that eclipses are temporary phenomena, after which life goes on again as before. But Tendryakov gives us no hint that Maya's infatuation with Gosha is a temporary one. On the contrary, her rejection of her husband is clearly symbolical of many young people's rejection of the materialism of Soviet society, and Gosha is the first stage in Maya's journey in search of spiritual satisfaction.

None of Tendryakov's heroes get as far as becoming churchgoers, although Yuri (in *On Apostolic Business*) reads the New Testament assiduously and has dreams in which he sees the Sea of Galilee and listens to Christ's sermon on the lilies of the field. Another author, Georgi Semyonov, goes further than this: the heroine of his story *The Ring Game*[6] has a dying vision of herself entering heaven and being received there by a Christ-figure. She is an old peasant woman, Anna Bogdashkina; we are not told whether she has ever been a religious believer, but we are given a detailed description of her miserable way of life, which she evidently hopes has earned her a place in heaven. Her husband was killed in the war; her only son grew up a no-good and is now serving a prison term for theft; and she lives alone in her hut in a deserted village, from which all the other inhabitants have moved to be nearer civilisation. Every few weeks she walks several kilometres through the forest to a road, where she catches an overcrowded bus to the nearest village shop. On the last occasion when she does this, the return bus is full up; she spends the night alone in the dark, sitting on the steps in front of the shop with her sack of provisions – and in the morning she is found there, dead. Dying, she has this final vision:

> Suddenly there was a steep, high staircase in front of her, and she was surprised to find herself easily climbing up the shining steps, up towards a golden-blue, heavenly glow of light . . .

> There were people around in bright clothing, who looked kindly at her and smiled encouragement . . . She felt she had known them always – especially one of them, who seemed to be the head man, and who surely must notice her soon, must see her looking at him . . . She gazed hard at him, trying to attract his attention, but he kept smiling and averting his gaze . . . Now she was at the top of the staircase, in a brightly-lit open space, surrounded on all sides by good and friendly people who . . . smilingly indicated that if that head man would only look at her, then she could stay there with them all. She wanted very much to stay, and she gazed entreatingly at him – until he suddenly relented and, still smiling that reserved and severe smile, lifted his eyes to hers . . .

Such an old-fashioned picture of paradise is unique in Soviet literature as far as I am aware; but the references to religion and believers are legion nowadays. In Svyatoslav Rybas's story *On Wheels*,[7] for instance, where the setting is a big car-service station (see pp. 63–4 above), there is a scene where the hero's mother-in-law is putting his son aged two to bed. She tells her daughter:

> 'When you put him down to sleep, make the sign of the cross over him and say, "Guardian Angel, save and be merciful to my son from evening till midnight, and from midnight till dawn." Then he'll sleep soundly, because his angel will guard him.'

In *The Wood-Grouse's Nest*,[8] a play by one of the most popular Soviet dramatists, Viktor Rozov, the setting is the luxurious Moscow flat of a big official in the world peace movement. He has a large collection of old icons, and one day he is horrified to find his desperately unhappy married daughter on her knees in front of them. She has had a good Soviet upper-class education, so she does not know how to cross herself – but she is praying: 'Help me, God, help me'.

Dmitri Kuzovlev, a retired *kolkhoz* chairman who now lives near Vologda, included many details of old religious customs still being observed today in an article about an old peasant carpenter, *Afonya's House*.[9] Afonya lived in an Old Believers' village, and although he and his wife were not believers, they lived according to their neighbours' customs: icons in every room, unpolished floors, no wallpaper. When he died, old Afonya was given an Old Believers' funeral: the body was laid on a bench in the house, with the head to the main icon, while old prayers were recited. At the last minute the body was coffined before being carried through the village; and over the grave in the Old Believers' cemetery a wooden cross was erected with the words 'Rest in peace' (*Mir prakhu tvoemu*).

The Old Believers have fascinated several other contemporary writers. One year after Fyodor Abramov's death (in May 1983), the Leningrad literary magazine *Neva* published the text of a television interview which he had recorded in 1981.[10] Asked what the early influences on him had been, Abramov replied – my aunt Irinya. She was unmarried, only semi-literate, and spent her life going round their North Russian village from family to family, working for people with her Singer sewing-machine. She was an Old Believer, who knew by heart the church literature on the saints, the hymns, the Apocrypha stories. Abramov added: 'Listening to her, was my first teaching in goodness and morals.'

The leading novelist Yuri Bondarev, in his latest novel *The Game*,[11] has many references to the historical Old Believers. His film director hero, Krymov, has just finished a film whose final scenes were shot at the deserted town of Pustozersk in Siberia, where the seventeenth-century Old Believer martyr Avvakum was burnt at the Tsar's orders. And Bondarev ends the novel with a scene in which Krymov's wife Olga is walking towards him dressed as a nun, accompanied by the emaciated figure of Avvakum. Krymov, who spends most of his time throughout the novel pondering on the meaning of life, seems to feel that Avvakum symbolises the individual triumphing in opposition to dictatorship. This view of the Old Believers as dissidents worthy of admiration (but surely not of emulation?) is shared by a younger fictional heroine in the latest novel by Elena Katasonova.[12] A university lecturer on folklore, she has to organise a summer expedition by a group of her students who will go out into the field to collect folksongs and stories. She chooses to send them to the Lake Onega area, because this part of Russia has an old tradition of freedom, shown by the fact that the institution of serfdom never spread there, and by the presence of the descendants of religious émigrés such as the Old Believers.

Much more widespread among writers than this interest in old Russian religious sects is their fascination with the buildings which believers erected in the past, so many of which are now in ruins. The campaign for the preservation of old churches and monasteries is supported with great enthusiasm by many declaredly atheist writers. But this passion can sometimes lead them into trouble, as was recently demonstrated in the case of Vladimir Soloukhin (see also chapter 7 above). In February 1982 this well-known writer was reproved by the Party magazine *Kommunist* for allowing religious motifs to creep into his writings. Several readers had written to *Kommunist* to protest at the following passage, which occurs in a collection of literary jottings which Soloukhin had published in *Nash Sovremennik*:[13]

> In this twentieth century, no sensible man can possibly have any doubt that there exists in this world, in the Universe, in the variety of life on earth, a higher, reasonable element. For if no such element exists, then we would have to suppose that such complex and accurate organisations as a flower (or plant), a bird, a man, a human brain, had each of them appeared as a result of some happy coincidence, some blind unprogrammed fusion of various chemical elements, molecules and atoms. But exact and complex instruments like the kidneys, the heart, the thyroid gland, the ear-drum, the eye, not to mention the chromosomes, could not have arisen blindly, on their own. All these organs work according to the reasoned laws of mathematics, chemistry, physics. The main question today is not, does a higher form of reason exist? but – does this higher reason know about me, and does it care about me at all?

Some of the letters to *Kommunist* about this passage protested that Soloukhin 'is clearly playing around with the idea of the existence of God'. His arguments, one engineer reader pointed out, are the same as those used by church leaders in defence of religion, and they are quite unworthy of a Soviet writer who is a Communist Party member. The editors of *Kommunist* agreed with this criticism, and in a later issue the magazine printed a report of a

Party meeting of the Moscow poets' group of the Writers' Union, at which Soloukhin was officially reproved. He assured the meeting that he has always been and still is a convinced atheist, and regretted that he had included 'careless phrases' in his writings which had given readers cause to criticise him.

Despite these protestations, two conclusions from the Soloukhin case seem to me inescapable: firstly, this Soviet 'establishment' author is extremely bothered by the question of the existence of God; and secondly, the authorities still care very much that writers should appear to be atheists, since they see any public acknowledgment of the existence of a Deity as a direct threat to the basis of the regime.

REFERENCES

1 Daniil Granin, *Kartina* (*Novy Mir* 1980, nos. 1–2).
2 Daniil Granin, *Voprosy i otvety* (*Oktyabr* 1981, no. 9).
3 Vladimir Tendryakov, *Chudotvornaya* (*Znamya* 1958, no. 5).
4 Vladimir Tendryakov, *Apostol'skaya komandirovka* (*Nauka i Religiya* 1969, nos. 8–10).
5 Vladimir Tendryakov, *Zatmenie* (*Druzhba Narodov* 1977, no. 5).
6 Georgi Semyonov, *Igra v kolechko* (*Nash Sovremennik* 1982, no. 7).
7 Svyatoslav Rybas, *Na kolyosakh* (*Oktyabr* 1981, no. 10).
8 Viktor Rozov, *Gnezdo glukharya* (*Teatr* 1979, no. 2).
9 Dmitri Kuzovlev, *Afonin dom* (*Nash Sovremennik* 1981, no. 10).
10 Fyodor Abramov, Television interview from 1981 (*Neva* 1984, no. 5).
11 Yuri Bondarev, *Igra* (*Novy Mir* 1985, nos. 1–2).
12 Elena Katasonova, *Bab'i vek* (*Neva* 1985, nos. 7–8).
13 Vladimir Soloukhin, *Kameshki na ladoni* (*Nash Sovremennik* 1981, no. 3).

Postscript

The evidence put forward in the preceding chapters would seem to indicate that Soviet men and women possess much the same assortment of virtues and vices as do citizens of any other contemporary state. There exists, however, this difference: the Soviet regime has plans for changing both people's behaviour and their psychological make-up in the near future. The Party Central Committee Secretary, Konstantin Chernenko, told a Party Plenum in June 1983: 'The revolutionary transformation of society is impossible without changing man himself. And our Party proceeds from the premise that the moulding of the new man is not only the most important aim but also an imperative condition of communist construction.'

By 'moulding', the Party leaders seem to mean strengthening the workers' sense of conscience (an honest day's work for an honest day's pay), organising them better so as to get more out of them (everywhere in Russia slogans are to be seen – 'More production from less workers!'), and stiffening their determination to improve life here and now by bombarding them with atheist propaganda (which tries to remove all hope of anything better in the next world). Some authors are already writing stories about 'positive heroes', the 'new men' who show many of the admirable qualities which the Party would like to encourage. But in some cases these heroes' efforts to better themselves by hard and honest labour are bringing them into conflict with the authorities.

One such conflict is the basis of a recent novel by Anatoli Pristavkin, *The Sub-Town*, published in *Novy Mir* in 1983.[1] The hero, a young engineer named Grigori Shokhov, has spent several years working at various big building sites. Now he arrives at the site of a new town on a northern river, and decides to settle down for good, build a house, and install his family in it. He comes of peasant stock and thinks a man is no good without his own home.

Pristavkin makes it clear that Shokhov is far from being a petty-bourgeois or *meshchanin*: he believes in hard work, and in people taking pleasure in their own good workmanship rather than working just for money. But he also believes in a highly individualist reward for his hard work: a house of his own, with a high fence all round it:

> A fence gives you the chance to stand on your own ground . . . You come home after work, and there are your own flower-beds, trees, a dog, small livestock of various kinds, even sparrows. And you are the tsar here, the king, the president, the head of everything – and that makes you a full person! Maybe you're pushed around at work, people are rude to you on the way home, they swear at you in the shops – but once you've come through your own gate and put the latch down, you're your own man, no one will offend you or shout at you or touch you. You can throw out your chest, take your shirt off, let your skin and lungs have a rest; your heart beats more quietly, your nerves settle down, you feel yourself a man again!

The official policy in this new town is against allowing people to put up their own dwellings, whether temporary or permanent; they are supposed to live in workers' hostels until flats are available for them in new blocks. Shokhov ignores this: he finds a fellow-individualist named Petrukha who is already living in a home-made shack, and the two of them spend all their spare time building Shokhov a house. Petrukha is an oddball with a mystery past, who has no regard for material values. His philosophy is:

> The main thing is not to get in the way of anyone else's way of life – let them live how they want to . . . Each of us must work honestly and thus bring happiness for all . . . If anyone comes and starts telling me how I ought to live, that's a bad thing: people have different ideas of happiness, and my idea is that no one should impose their sort of happiness on me . . .

Shokhov agrees with him. Indeed, he goes further: 'If you want happiness, don't wait for it to come, but build it yourself.' But such militant individualism is too much for the local authorities, especially when Shokhov's example is followed by dozens of single workers and families. They all put up temporary shacks outside the new town, forming a whole settlement known locally as *Vor-gorodok* ('the thieves' sub-town' – because the building materials were all obtained unofficially, i.e. stolen from the State). The author Pristavkin's sympathies are clearly all with the inhabitants of *Vor-gorodok:* they are not parasites or speculators, he points out, but good working-class lads, many of them future leading workers or even managers. But their venture comes to nothing; a town plan has been agreed at a high level, the site of Shokhov's house has been scheduled for a future banana store, and Shokhov himself is put in charge of levelling the shanty town. The novel ends with him driving a bulldozer to flatten his own house.

Judging by this example, individualism is still a force to be reckoned with, and one that may well militate against the regime's attempts to mould the 'new Soviet man'. Some Soviet individuals even resent the moulding process so much that they drop right out of society. An example of this occurs in *A Gap in the Calendar*, a novel by Iosif Gerasimov.[2] In it a steelworks director tells the story of a factory manager who, after a successful career putting his factory back on its feet after the war, suddenly realised that the pressures were too great and top management was not for him – so he got out:

> This man Zakhvatkin was a good chap, a specialist who had studied abroad in America . . . He got his factory going, built workers' housing, and everyone at Dutov liked him. And then suddenly, a man like that goes and chucks it all up. They didn't want to let him go, but he insisted on resigning, and went off to Lake Baikal to catch fish. I couldn't believe it when I heard about it, and I thought – when I take my holiday, I'll go and see how he's living now. I flew to Irkutsk and then went on by boat, and I found Zakhvatkin. He's head of a small fisherman's co-operative. He's grown a beard and wears boots and a canvas smock – and he's beaming with happiness, fit to burst with it. He lives with his wife and two children in a big peasant hut – and outside there's the *taiga* for him to go hunting in. He has herbs, mushrooms, berries – and fish. I kept asking him: 'What

made you suddenly give up the factory and come out here?' 'Well,' he said, 'I've dreamt all my life of living like this, and I suddenly realised that I would never make the dream come true unless I broke out of that charmed circle.' 'But surely your true place isn't here?' I said to him. He just laughed: '*Here* I am at home,' he said, 'it was *there* that I was out of place.' And I realised that he really has moved out there for good.

At the end of this story, the steelworks director asks a very Tolstoyan question, and one that must be anathema to official educators and moulders: 'Perhaps *that's* how one really ought to live?'

REFERENCES

1 Anatoli Pristavkin, *Gorodok* (*Novy Mir* 1983, nos. 1–2).
2 Iosif Gerasimov, *Probel v kalendare* (*Novy Mir* 1983, no. 3).

Bibliography

The following are the main Soviet literary periodicals, from which the source material for this book was taken. All are published monthly, with considerable variations both in their print runs and their editorial policies.

Druzhba Narodov
Organ of the USSR Writers' Union, founded 1939.
Editor: Sergei Baruzdin. *Circulation*: 155,000.
Specialises in the writings of Soviet authors of non-Russian nationality, which it publishes in Russian translation, but also has its own regular Russian authors such as Tendryakov, Trifonov, Okudjava, Baklanov.

Molodaya Gvardiya
Organ of the Komsomol Central Committee, founded 1922.
Editor: Anatoli Ivanov. *Circulation*: 650,000.
The main Russian nationalist organ: dominated by an extreme right-wing group in the late 1960s, but since 1970 has been more moderate. Its regular authors before 1971 included Proskurin and Soloukhin, both of whom now publish elsewhere.

Moskva
Organ of the RSFSR Writers' Union and the Moscow Writers' Organisation, founded 1957.
Editor: Mikhail Alekseyev. *Circulation*: 500,000.

Nash Sovremennik
Organ of the RSFSR Writers' Union, founded by Gorky in 1933.
Editor: S. V. Vikulov. *Circulation*: 220,000.
The organ of the moderate nationalists, its authors include Belov

(since 1979), Proskurin (since 1982), Rasputin (since 1974), Soloukhin (since 1982).

Neva
Organ of the RSFSR Writers' Union and the Leningrad Writers' Organisation, founded 1955.
Editor: B. N. Nikolsky. *Circulation*: 290,000.

Novy Mir
Organ of the USSR Writers' Union, founded 1925.
Editor: Vladimir Karpov. *Circulation*: 420,000.
Traditionally the most liberal of the journals. During the two periods of Tvardovsky's editorship (1950–4 and 1958–70), published works by such controversial writers as Dombrovsky, Grossman, Ovechkin, Solzhenitsyn, Vladimov, Voinovich. Its recent regular authors include Abramov, Belov (before 1970), Aitmatov, Dorosh, Geiko, Granin, Kashtanov, Lipatov, Shukshin, Tendryakov, Trifonov (until 1975), Vladimov, Yashin, Zalygin (up to 1967).

Oktyabr
Organ of the RSFSR Writers' Union, founded 1924.
Editor: A. A. Ananiev. *Circulation*: 175,000.
Traditionally a hard-line conservative journal. Regular authors include Adamyan, Kaverin.

Teatr
Organ of the USSR Writers' Union and the USSR Ministry of Culture, founded 1937.
Editor: G. Borovik. *Circulation*: 32,600.

Yunost
Organ of the USSR Writers' Union, founded 1955.
Editor: Andrei Dementiev. *Circulation*: 3,300,000.
Aimed at young readers.

Znamya
Organ of the USSR Writers' Union, founded 1931.
Editor: Yu. Voronov. *Circulation*: 250,000.

Notes on Writers

These notes are necessarily incomplete, since personal data on Soviet authors are hard to come by and even harder to check, and only the more important writers quoted are included. The works listed are those by which they are mainly known: I have not attempted to include all their published fiction.

ABRAMOV, Fyodor (1920–83)
Born in a peasant family in the Archangel region.
The Pryaslin novel cycle: *Brat'ya i sestry* (1958); *Dve zimy i tri leta* (1968); *Puti i pereput'ya* (1973); *Dom* (1978).
Stories: *Vokrug da okolo* (1963); *Pelageya* (1969); *Mamonikha* (1980).

ANANIEV, Anatoli (1925–)
Editor of *Oktyabr*. Born in Djambul, Kazakhstan; fought in war with distinction.
Novels: *Tanki idut rombom* (1963); *Versty lyubvi* (1971); *Gody bez voiny* (1975–81).
Anti-religious essays: *Ten' Iisusa* (1961). Anti-religious story: *Kozyri monakha Grigoriya* (1964).

BAKLANOV, Grigori (1923–)
Born in Voronezh, fought in the war, then studied at Gorky Literary Institute in Moscow, where he was a pupil of Paustovsky. His early stories were about the war; later ones more concerned with the heroes' psychology.
Stories: *Pyad zemli* (1959); *Mertvye sramu ne imut* (1961); *Men'shi sredi bratiev* (1981); *Vot i konchilas' voina* (1982).
Novel: *Druzya* (1975).

BELOV, Vasili (1932–)

A native of Vologda, he has worked on a *kolkhoz* and in a Urals factory, and has been writing since 1956, usually about the life of Northern Russian peasants.

Stories: *Plotnitskie rasskazy* (1968); *Bukhtiny Vologodskie* (1969); *Privychnoe delo* (1966).

Novel: *Kanuny* (1972–6, set in a village in 1928).

Essays: *Lad: ocherki po narodnoi estetike* (1979–81).

DOROSH, Efim (1908–72)

Born in Kirovograd, trained as an artist, early stories about the civil war. Author of a writer's diary, containing comments on peasant characters, customs and agricultural methods in the area not far south of Moscow during the years 1954–70. Also wrote on medieval Russian art and architecture.

Diary: *Derevensky dnevnik* (published 1956–70).

On old Russian art: *Razmyshleniya v Zagorske* (1967); *Rostovsky Kreml* (1967); *Zhivoe derevo iskusstva* (1967); *Obrazy Rossii* (1969).

GEIKO, Yuri (1948–)

Published his first story while on army service; as a Lieutenant, he was stationed in the Kazakh steppe, guarding a well. After the army, studied at the Gorky Literary Institute.

Stories: *Na kolodtse* (1973); *Zapakhi detstva* (1978); *Saiga* (1980); *Ispytanie* (1983).

GRANIN, Daniil (1918–)

Real name German. Son of a forester, he trained as an engineer in Leningrad, and has been writing since 1949. Usually writes about scientists or technicians, but in his last novel has broken new ground. Author of a documentary book on the Leningrad blockade (with A. Adamovich).

Novels: *Iskateli* (1955); *Posle svad'by* (1959); *Idu na grozu* (1962); *Kartina* (1980).

Documentary: *Blokadnaya Kniga* (1977).

Stories: *Kto-to dolzhen* (1970, collection).

KARELIN, Lazar (1920–)
Author of stories, novels, scenarios; an anti-Israel article (1970); travel notes (1983, on Helsinki).
Novels: *Mikro-raion* (1962); *Zemletryasenie* (1969, on the Ashkhabad earthquake of 1948).
Stories: *Golovokruzhenie* (1971); *Roditel'skoe sobranie* (1976); *Seismicheski poyas* (1979); *Zmeyelov* (1982); *Posledni pereulok* (1984).

KASHTANOV, A. (1938–)
An engineer by training, studied in Moscow and later worked in Minsk.
Stories: *Zavodskoi raion* (1973); *Belye doma Tolochi* (1974); *Korobeiniki* (1981).

KRON, Alexander (1909–83)
During the war, edited a Baltic submariners' newspaper and was also a front-line correspondent. First became well known by his play, *Naval Officer*, written in Leningrad during the blockade.
Novels: *Dom i korabl* (1964, on the blockade); *Bessonitsa* (1977).
Plays: *Glubokaya razvedka* (1941, about Baku oilmen); *Ofitser flota* (1944); *Kandidat Partii* (1950).
Documentary story: *Kapitan dal'nevo plavaniya* (on the ace submariner Marinesco, 1983).

LIPATOV, Vil (1927–79)
A native of Siberia, his stories are usually set there.
Stories: *Shestero* (1958); *Strezhen* (1961); *Cherny Yar* (1963); *Povest bez nazvaniya, syuzheta i kontsa* (1978).
Film scenarios: *Inzhener Pronchatov* (1972); *Derevensky detektiv* (1967).

NAGIBIN, Yuri (1920–)
Born in Moscow, fought and was wounded in the war, then became a war correspondent for *Trud*. Since the war has written stories, essays, scenarios.
Recent stories: *Dorozhnoe proisshestvie* (1980); *Terpenie* (1982, about a war cripple); *Rachmaninov* (1983, biographical).

NILIN, Pavel (1908–81)
Born in Irkutsk, where his father had been exiled. Before the war, worked as a journalist in Irkutsk; during the war was a *Pravda* correspondent. Author of plays, novels, stories, several of which have been successfully filmed.
Stories: *Zhestokost* (1956, about policemen and bandits in Siberia in the early 1920s); *Dur* (1973); *Vpervye zamuzhem* (1978).
Play: *Na belom svete* (1947).
Scenarios: *Bolshaya zhizn* (1940, 1958); *Zhestokost* (1958); *Ispytatelny srok* (1960); *Cherez kladbishche* (1965).

PROSKURIN, Pyotr (1928–)
From a peasant family in Bryansk region, he worked as driver and woodcutter; after army service he worked in a Kamchatka *lespromkhoz* in 1955–8, and then lived in Khabarovsk, where his first stories were published. In 1962 he went to Moscow to study at the Gorky Literary Institute, and remained there.
Novels: *Glubokie rany* (1960); *Gor'kie travy* (1964); *Kamen' serdolik* (1968); *Sud'ba* (1972); *Imya tvoyo* (1978, religious theme).
Autobiographical essay: *Slovom ne ubii* (1982).

RASPUTIN, Valentin (1937–)
Born in Irkutsk region, he started as a journalist in Siberia.
Stories: *Den'gi dlya Marii* (1968); *Posledni srok* (1971); *Zhivi i pomni* (1974); *Proshchanie s Matyoroi* (1974); *Vek zhivi – vek lyubi* (1982); *Pozhar* (1985).

SHUKSHIN, Vasili (1929–74)
Born in a peasant family in the Altai region, he had 7-year schooling and then worked on *kolkhozy* and building sites until service in the Soviet Navy. Then went to the Moscow Cinema Institute, where he studied under Mikhail Romm. After this he had a triple career as actor, film director and writer, until his early death from a heart attack. Much loved for his stories about peasant life, which are deeply patriotic and yet extremely frank about poverty and deprivation. His bestknown story, *Kalina krasnaya* (1973, about an ex-criminal's doomed attempt to go straight), became a very successful film.

SHTEMLER, Ilya (1933–)
Born in Baku, trained as a geophysicist, then worked as an engineer in Leningrad, where he now lives.
Novels: *Grossmeisterski bal* (1965); *Takso-park* (1980); *Univermag* (1982); *Utrennee shosse* (1983).

SOLOUKHIN, Vladimir (1924–)
Born in Vladimir region, he graduated from the Gorky Literary Institute in 1951. Poet, writer of lyrical prose about the countryside, novelist, campaigner for the preservation of old Russian art and architecture. A Party member since 1952, he has twice been officially accused of being a Christian – by Kochetov in his novel in 1969, and by the magazine *Kommunist* in 1982.
Novel: *Mat-machekha* (1964).
Essays: *Vladimirskie prosyolki* (1957, translated into English as *Walks in Rural Russia*); *Kaplya rosy* (1960); *Pis'ma iz Russkovo Muzeya* (1966, on art); *Chornye doski* (1969, on collecting icons); *Kameshki na ladoni* (1967–82), *Vremya sobirat' kamni* (1980) and *Prodolzhenie vremeni* (1982) – random jottings, mostly on art.

TENDRYAKOV, Vladimir (1923–84)
A native of Vologda region, he fought in the war and was wounded, came to Moscow in 1945, graduated from the Gorky Literary Institute in 1951 (pupil of Paustovsky). Author of many long stories, of which the early works are set in the countryside and the later ones mainly concerned with urban young people and their upbringing.
His best-known works:
On religious themes: *Chudotvornaya* (1958); *Apostol'skaya komandirovka* (1969); *Zatmenie* (1977).
On country problems: *Ukhaby* (1956); *Podyonka – vek korotki* (1965); *Konchina* (1968, on collectivisation).
On youthful crime: *Rasplata* (1979).
Plays: *Bely flag* (1962); *Sovet da lyubov* (1973).
Scenarios: *Chuzhaya rodnya* (1956); *Chudotvornaya* (1960); *Sud* (1961).
Novel: *Za begushchim dnyom* (1959).

TRIFONOV, Yuri (1925–81)
Born in Moscow, worked in an aircraft factory during the war, then attended the Gorky Literary Institute (under Paustovsky) from which he graduated in 1949, awarded a State Prize for his first novel in 1950. His father, a Party official, was arrested and executed in 1937. His basic theme: moral principles of the intelligentsia.
Novels: *Studenty* (1950); *Utolenie zhazhdy* (1963, on building of the Turkmen canal); *Otblesk kostra* (1965, on his father's Civil War experiences); *Neterpenie* (1973, on Zhelyabov); *Starik* (1978); *Vremya i mesto* (1981, published posthumously).
Stories: *Obmen* (1969); *Predvaritel'nye itogi* (1970); *Dolgoe proshchanie* (1971); *Drugaya zhizn* (1975); *Dom na naberezhnoi* (1976).

TVARDOVSKY, Alexander (1910–71)
Son of a village blacksmith in Smolensk region. As a poet, best known for his Soviet soldier's epic, *Vasili Tyorkin* (1945), and its sequel, *Tyorkin na tom svete* (written 1953, published 1963); also for many short lyrical poems, and for the long *Strana Muravia* (1936) and *Dom u Dorogi* (1946). Two spells as editor of *Novy Mir*, 1950–4 and 1958–70; thanks to him, many of the best works of post-war Soviet literature were published, by such controversial authors as Dombrovsky, Grossman, Ovechkin, Solzhenitsyn, Vladimov, Voinovich.

VASILIEV, Boris
A prolific writer, one of whose war stories, *A zori zdes tikhie* (1969), became a successful film.
Novels: *Ne strelyaite v belykh lebedei* (1973); *Byli i nebyli* (1977–8, about the Russo-Turkish war).
Stories: *Velikolepnaya shestyorka* (1980); *Vy chie, starichie?* (1982, on old people's problems).

VLADIMOV, Georgi (1931–)
Born in Kharkov, son of a schoolteacher, read law at Leningrad University. From 1967 onwards, protested against the treatment of dissident writers; in 1977 became secretary of the Moscow branch of Amnesty International. Emigrated in 1983 to West Germany.

Novels: *Bolshaya ruda* (1961); *Tri minuty molchaniya* (1969 – a fuller version published in English as *Three Minutes' Silence*, in 1985); *Verny Ruslan* (1975, published in West Germany by *Grani*).

YASHIN, Alexander (1913–68)
Born in Vologda, fought in the war, left the Gorky Literary Institute in 1951. Lyrical poet, and author of several stories, one of which (*Rychagi*, 1956) got him some criticism for his negative portrayal of village Communists. A later story, *Vologodskaya svad'ba* (1962), was also criticised for too much realism. He settled in his native, remote Vologda village, where he died.

ZALYGIN, Sergei (1931–   )
Born in a village in the Bashkir Republic, studied at an agricultural technicum and the Omsk Agricultural Institute. Worked as hydrologist and engineer; has been writing since 1941; now lives in Moscow.
Novels: *Tropy Altaya* (1962); *Solyonaya Pad* (1967, on civil war in Siberia); *Komissiya* (1975, on collectivisation); *Posle buri* (1980–2, set in Siberia in the 1920s).
Story: *Na Irtyshe* (1964, on collectivisation).
Since 1969 has been one of the secretaries of the RSFSR Writers' Union.

Index